THINGS I WISH I'D KNOWN AT 13: OR MAYBE EVEN SOONER

A GIRL'S GUIDE TO GIRL STUFF

Sonja Reynolds

Author's Tranquility Press
MARIETTA, GEORGIA

Copyright © 2021 by Sonja Reynolds

All rights reserved. No part of this publication may be reproduced, distributed or transmitted in any form or by any means, including photocopying, recording, or other electronic or mechanical methods, without the prior written permission of the publisher, except in the case of brief quotations embodied in critical reviews and certain other noncommercial uses permitted by copyright law. For permission requests, write to the publisher, addressed "Attention: Permissions Coordinator," at the address below.

Sonja Reynolds/Author's Tranquility Press
2706 Station Club Drive SW
Marietta, GA 30060
www.authorstranquilitypress.com

Ordering Information:
Quantity sales. Special discounts are available on quantity purchases by corporations, associations, and others. For details, contact the "Special Sales Department" at the address above.

Things I Wish I'd Known At 13: Or Maybe Even Sooner
A Girl's Guide To Girl Stuff/ Sonja Reynolds
Hardback   ISBN: 978-1-956480-99-3
Paperback   ISBN: 978-1-7376993-9-2
Ebook   ISBN: 978-1-957208-00-8

This is dedicated to all the girls who feel like Aliens. You are not alone. You are Worthy. And you are LOVED.

"If you're always trying to be NORMAL, you will never know how AMAZING you can be"

—- Maya Angelou

WHY I CREATED THIS GUIDE

There are things I feel every female should be taught as they grow into young women, things they will value their entire lives. It would seem like common sense that the most important and especially sensitive things females should know would come from the females closest to them. But sometimes, that just doesn't happen, and the information comes from people you meet on your journey through life. I've had some wonderful female mentors, teachers, friends and role models over the years who've helped me through things only another female can. When I worked as a youth counselor for teenaged females it made me understand the importance of having someone to provide wisdom, encouragement and guidance. I was able to provide these things by sharing my life experiences with many young women. One of the greatest rewards was later having some of those young women retell my stories or tell me how much my sharing meant to them and had changed their lives.

With the use of technology, especially cell phones, people have lost some basic communication skills over the years. Many people don't even like to talk, they would rather text or send an email. But so much is lost in translation with these methods. I've seen campaign ads recently that promote talking to teens, "Talk to your teens, they're listening" is one of those. My belief is that young people truly want to be guided, even though they may act like they don't and rebel and fight against it at times. But when they don't get this guidance at all, or see that adults are reluctant to address certain things or worse avoid any conflict or difficult situations at all by just giving them whatever they want or turning a blind eye, teens lose even more respect for adults. So, I felt the need to find a way to provide some of this guidance in a format that's easy to access, understand, share and use. They are things I would readily communicate to any young woman I'd meet, and if I had a daughter, it's what we would talk about. They are things I wish had been shared with me when I was developing into a young woman.

A Quick Note

I read through the Guide many times before finally submitting it for print. However...there may be times where I repeat myself. If you see that, it just means that a particular subject was REALLY important to me. While reading and editing sometimes I'd think of something and write a chapter, then go back and see that I'd already said something about that subject. But the newer chapter had a different "flavor" so to speak, and I didn't want to take it out.

You may not agree with some of the things I have to say. This is totally fine and really another reason I chose to write this. This book is a tool; its purpose is to get you to think about things and make decisions about how you feel about those things and maybe make plans and choices that help you understand yourself better. The subjects can be used in many different ways and I'd hope that you share the book with people you know and talk about these things, debate on them, analyze them and maybe find some solutions. The ultimate goal I hope, is that it causes you to purposefully make positive decisions about some very important things in your young life that will affect you when you are an adult.

What's Inside

- A Weighty Situation: the issue of eating disorders
- Are You My Mother: family connections
- Be A Part Of Something: being involved
- Blenders, Skillets and Serving Spoons: problem solving tools
- Caught In The Net: dangers of the Internet
- Dance Lessons: what you do on the dancefloor
- Dead Presidents: choosing your income
- Defending The Temple: rights to your body
- Eyes on the Prize: the love game
- Fashion Police: what you wearing says about you
- Filling The Gaps: knowing the Creator
- Guiding Light: listening to your inner voice
- Handle Your Business: building business sense
- Hills, Valleys and Depressions: emotional ups and downs
- I'm Every Woman: knowing your body
- Is It In You: your environment's influence
- Just Say No: opting out on drugs
- Leather and Filled With Sand: physical abuse
- Let's Face It: what you show the world

- Lip Service: communication skills
- Lost and Found: life and relationships
- Making Up: cosmetics and you
- Mama Oh No Not Mia: being a young mom, or not
- Move Your Body: getting fit
- Passion's Fruit: living your dreams
- Seeds Of Doubt: impact of dishonesty
- So Fresh So Clean: personal hygiene
- Tech NOoooo: disconnecting from tech devices
- The Devil's Workshop: boredom's booby-traps
- The Joneses: traps of material things
- The Process: grieving the loss of a loved one
- The Wrong Prince: bad boyfriends
- To Thine Own Self Be True: believing in yourself
- Watch Your Mouth: what you speak into your life
- What's Wrong With A Virgin: the option of waiting
- Who Are These People: homelife headaches
- Who Do you Love: appreciating yourself
- Work It Out: being a good employee
- Pushed to the End/The Wrong End: bullies and suicide

A Weighty Situation

There are so many reasons females end up with eating disorders, like:
- Wanting to look like the model images they see on TV, magazines, etc.
- A sense of control: if they can't control some particular area of their lives they feel maybe they can at least control their weight
- Depression
- Anger
- Resentment
- Peer Pressure

There are also a number of different kinds of eating disorders. My goal is not to go into a bunch of medical terms and facts, those are things you can find in a variety of places: the Internet, library, school nurse, and your doctor.

When I say "disorder" I mean eating habits that are way *out* of "order". For example, are you eating too much, too often, when you aren't even hungry? Are you hiding food, thinking about it more than anything else? Or on the other hand are you eating and then making yourself throw it up? Has your clothing size dropped significantly and you still feel "fat"? Any of the resources I listed above can give you lists of behaviors that may determine whether you have a problem. But ultimately your doctor is the one that can diagnose an eating disorder, but you need to identify the problem and accept the need for help. My goal here is to let you know that you don't need to drive yourself crazy trying to fit into somebody *else's* body.

Did you know that the average woman is a size 12? I get a bit frustrated when I go shopping because there are always a bunch of sizes 4, 6, and 8 on the rack and all the 10s and up are missing! You would think that clothing stores would make sure that they stay stocked up on the highest selling sizes. But no! I bet that's the cause of some ladies saying, "Well, maybe I should be those small sizes and then I wouldn't have a problem finding clothes". Hey, don't even go that route. Just ask when the next shipment will come in, complain about it to the manager if necessary or just go to another store.

Being able to be happy with the way you look is sometimes an ongoing and difficult process. You may gain some weight and then feel you need to lose it. That's fine if you do it in a healthy way like exercising or making changes to your eating habits. There are also many different kinds of diets out there; a new one seems to pop up every day. All diets are not healthy, even if they claim to be safe or you find them in a health food store.

By the time I left full time military I had gained over 15 pounds. I exercised very little because I didn't have to do it daily. Then I just couldn't stand it anymore. I was quickly approaching a larger clothing size and couldn't get into most of my old clothes! I don't like to shop for clothes very much, I like to buy stuff that will last a long time and not go out of style. I was about to have to buy all new stuff! I had tried a number of different diets while I was still full time military and I found that the only thing that really worked was changing my food intake and being more active. My first job out of the military was working at a wilderness education program that required a lot of physical energy, so it was easy to find ways to exercise. We walked over a mile a day anyway, so I took advantage of that. I also made sure I ate *slowly*. It takes your stomach time to realize that you are eating. People tend to eat quickly when they are hungry and then overeat because they don't feel full until it's too late. If you eat slowly and give your stomach time to figure out that you're eating, you will find that you are usually full before you finish your meal. The last thing I did was drink lots of water! I can't emphasize enough the importance of drinking water; it jump starts your metabolism (natural fat burning), it helps eliminate waste, helps your complexion, restores cells, and it's over 70% of your body composition. The water you lose with simply daily activity needs to be replenished. So, within 3 months I lost 15 lbs! It dropped off little by little each week until I was looking and feeling the best I had in years! Notice I said within 3 MONTHS, not 3 days or weeks. That's 5 pounds a month. Most people don't want to wait that long and jump into a fast acting diet. But it has been shown that people that lose weight slowly and in a healthy, natural way tend to keep it off. Keep in mind, I was also in my 30s and it's harder for some women to lose weight when they are older. So, if I could do it, so can you! Take time to learn what causes you to gain weight, what foods, what circumstances, what emotions. Knowing these things is key in deciding what actions to take if you want to lose weight.

We are all created in God's image, and that's a beautiful thing. We were not all meant to be a size 4 and it's senseless to think that if you aren't a size 4 something is wrong with you. Are you healthy? Now, that's what's important. If you're healthy you're probably right where you need to be as far as your body shape and weight, even if it doesn't fit the picture you have of the perfect body.

I used to hate my arms. They looked so fat when I'd see them in pictures of myself. They were muscular from exercise and work, but once the muscles were relaxed my arms just looked fat to me and I hated it. Then one day I was going through my photo albums and found a picture of my mom and discovered that I had arms just like my mom! I realized I was supposed to have the arms I had and that they were beautiful, just like moms. Genetics play a role in what you look like and if you see a pattern in body shapes within your family you should understand that there are just some things a diet won't help: the shape of your head, the color of your eyes, the size of your feet, or sometimes even your butt! So start finding ways to love what you have and if there's something you can change in a healthy way, then, handle your business. Never be afraid to ask someone to help you. If you have a friend that's going through the same issues, team up and fight the battle together. Keep in mind that real beauty comes from within and you just have to take care of the packaging.

Let's Get the Skinny:
- How do you feel about your weight?
- If it is a struggle for you, what things have you done to improve it? What things have you noticed actually work?
- Do you match your family's typical body shape, meaning: does your body look like other people in your family?
- Are you setting realistic goals for yourself when trying to lose weight? Realistic being a few pounds a month...not per week.
- If you have a doctor, what has he or she said about your overall health? Did they give you any instructions for follow? If so, have you followed them?
- How much exercise do you get on a regular basis? If not scheduled exercise, how about activity in general (walking for instance)

- What do you want your body to look like and is that image realistic based on your family history and your physical activity?

Are You My Mother?

One of my favorite books when I was little was about this little bird that had fallen out of its nest while its mother was away looking for worms. The little bird went looking for its mother. It searched all around coming in contact with a bunch of different animals asking them all if they were his mother. Because the bird had come out of his shell while his mother was away, it had no clue what she looked like, which was the reason for all the confusion.

I think many of us are on the same mission as that little bird: looking for our family. I'm not talking about literally looking for them like they are lost or have been taken away, I mean looking for a family in which we feel connected to and loved by. Many of us may have grown up in families that weren't the traditional mother, father, sister, or brother kind of thing. You may have grown up with aunts, uncles and cousins like I did, or grandparents or maybe even in a foster home. All of us have had some very different kinds of experiences being a part of our families, even the traditional ones.

You may feel like an alien in your own home. Your sense of style, your personality, your interests, may not match with anyone in your immediate home family. But that doesn't mean there's something wrong with you, it just makes you, YOU.

There were so many times that I wished someone from my family had been there when I was getting an award for an achievement or giving my all during a track meet. However there were people who were there during those victorious moments who did cheer for me when my team won a 400-meter relay that I anchored or told me how proud they were of me when I got my scholarship to college. Those people were like family sent from heaven. I could seek out these same people for advice and a shoulder to cry on even after I left high school. They were lifelines for me. Even if I did something stupid and they lit into me about it, I respected and loved them for their time and the caring they showed me.

It's always hard for me when I see young ladies going all out to get the attention of their families and not getting support when they need it. Sometimes that was their reason to start doing things that were dangerous or illegal. When I was working with some of these young women they would ask me over and over, what they were doing wrong or simply why their families didn't give them the support they felt they deserved or needed. I couldn't always answer their questions, but I did tell them this: sometimes the "family" you need may be found *outside* of the family you have.

Trusting an adult to be my friend was very valuable to me as a teenager. They kept me in line when I complained about situations going on at my house. They helped me see the other side to things, the grown up side. They gave me wisdom when my own failed me. And they were safe. By safe, I mean my family knew where I was and that I was in good hands when I left the house to spend time with them. It was often my friend's parents that I became closest to and sought out when I needed to talk to someone about big problems. Some of my teachers were also "friends" for me. They encouraged me and helped me see things I was good at and also challenged me when they saw I was looking for the easy way out of some thing because I was scared. They helped build and boost my self-esteem and confidence.

Yes, I know it's discouraging to not have the connections or relationships you want at home, but you also need to look at your part in those disconnections and relationships. How much time do you spend with your family? Do you run out on them when they want to have family time together? Do you support things they have interests in? Keep in mind that just because the things your family plans don't particularly interest you doesn't mean it's okay for you to not participate. Those plans are important to them, and their feelings are just as important as yours. A family is a very special kind of animal and should be given the best of care in order for it to be healthy. Feed it, nurture it, clean it when it needs it, take care of it when it's sick, pamper it, pet it, hold and squeeze it, and love it if you expect it to be there and do the same for you. Try not to expect more from your family than *you* are willing to give *them*. And understand that sometimes you won't always get the results you plan on, or the same treatment you feel you deserve.

I have learned that often you have to show people how you want to be loved, because they may assume they know what you want or need and be totally off base. Success with love and relationships involves lots of trial and error, but the biggest factor is communication. Communicate your needs with your family and allow them to do the same.

And so....?

Describe the relationship you have with the people you live with.

Does your relationship with them match up to your expectations of them? What can you do to help it if it's not like you feel it should be?

Are you doing anything that is unhealthy, illegal or unsafe in order to get your family's attention? Need an example: smoking, drugs, alcohol, sex, sneaking out, shop lifting, running way, not eating, over eating...should I go on? If you are doing some of these things, are you getting the results you want?

What makes you feel like you aren't connected or that you aren't getting the support you desire? Have you talked to your family about your concerns? Note: don't expect your family to be mind readers just because they know you. You have to voice your feelings sometimes in order for people to know what's going on. Read about communication in the *Lip Service* chapter.

If you feel you have a good connection with your family, what makes you feel that way? What kinds of things does your family do that makes everyone feel connected and important?

Try this one:

If your family agrees that there are some things that could be improved upon and are receptive to ideas, try organizing a "Family Night" if you don't already have one. Pick a particular day of every week that the family can get together and spend time really getting to know one another. It could be a time to play a game together, watch a movie, cook a meal together...be creative!

Be A Part Of Something

I used to be a runner. I would run away from just about everything. I didn't want to try to be a part of any particular group or association because I felt I didn't fit in. I didn't have an friend I felt were close and genuine. I felt awkward and out of place most of the time. I did try out for a few extracurricular things like Drill Team, basketball, volleyball, Flag team, but when I wasn't chosen for the teams, I thought that meant I wasn't cut out for it. So, then I started running away from things that required me being a part of a team. By thinking I wasn't cut out for certain things I created an imaginary separation between me and other kids and saw them as having some special talents I didn't have.

There were countless other organizations and groups I could have chosen to be involved in. I never really took advantage of the things my school had to offer that were more suited to my personality. I believed the sports associated groups to be the better groups to belong to. I wasn't wise enough to see the benefits of the Debate team, being on the yearbook staff, or being a class officer. I did briefly participate in some sport activities though. I completed a season of track in the 9th grade because my coach wouldn't allow me to quit when I got frustrated and tried to give up. Finishing that season was a valuable lesson for me because it allowed me to see that I had the ability to compete and win. My efforts with the tennis and volleyball team were not as fruitful and I kind of let it get to me.

But once I thought about what I really enjoyed and was good at I matched that up with the Art Club and the Vikettes. The Art Club is pretty self- explanatory; I socialized with other art students, compared projects and just got encouragement from the artsy crew. The Vikettes I will have to explain. Our school mascot was the Viking, and the Vikettes were a group of young women that were like hostesses. We tore tickets at the sports events, helped people find seats, and just generally helped out wherever help was needed. It was great because I got into all the games free and had the best seats. The teacher that organized the group chose me as a team leader at the first meeting! I guess she saw some leadership potential in me and that was a big booster for my self-esteem, and I guess prophetic because I have been in a number of other leadership roles since then, but that's another story.

So, although I didn't get a letter for my school jacket for being in these groups, I benefited from being a part of these groups. It gave me a start with learning how to work within a group and appreciation of being a part of something larger than myself. I gained some valuable interpersonal skills (working within a group skills), which are essential life tools. If you can't work within a team how many jobs do you think you will be able to hold? People with poor interpersonal skills don't often last in the workplace. They tend to wander from place to place blaming others for their problems unless they learn to improve their "people skills". So, unless you intend on being an at home entrepreneur you'd better take advantage of opportunities to develop interpersonal skills.

Colleges look for students who've been involved in organizations and groups, even those outside of school. College graduates applying for jobs have a better-looking resume when they can include a group or organization they were involved in, it lets the employer know they aren't afraid of being a part of a team. The closest I was to ever being a Girl Scout was eating the cookies, but the Scouts are a wonderful start to building those interpersonal skills. There are many other organizations outside of the school setting that will set you up for success as well;

volunteering at orphanages or churches, working with animals in shelters, and volunteering with disabled students.

So, get busy. Match your personality with a group or organization and start smoothing your pathway to interpersonal perfection! Even if a group looks interesting and doesn't really match your personality like you think it does, don't let that hold you back. Try it out, you never know, the Chess Team could be just what you need.

Think about it:
- What groups stir your interest, at school or otherwise?
- Do you know someone that's already a member of a particular group you find interesting that you could talk to?
- Are you afraid of being on a team? If so, why?
- If you've been a part of a team before, what benefits did it provide for you? If there were some bad parts, what were they and what can you do to deal with them in the future if they arise again?
- If you can't find a group or team you feel fits you, have you considered starting your own?

Blenders, Skillets and Serving Spoons

I like to cook, but I'm not a good enough cook that I can whip up all the stuff I really like without having to use a recipe. Once I decided to attempt cooking some of the things I like, I had to get some stuff to cook with; some real pots and pans, some measuring cups, a cutting board, and some good knives just for starters. The more I expanded my cooking experiences the more things I had to get for the kitchen to be able to prepare things. It's funny now when I look around my kitchen and see things I've never had to use in the past. And yet I know that there are still a lot of things I will need in the future because there are things I have yet to cook that I can't make with the things I have now. As well as things to cook with in the future, I will also need new things to serve the finished products.

When I was younger, I had to make lots of choices and decisions. As an adult I've had to make lots of decisions and choices too. What do you think would happen if I made the same choices and decisions as an adult that I did when I was a child? Let's say I had to plan a meal for a group of business partners, and I chose the things I would have liked when I was a child. Do you think my business partners would enjoy a meal of Spaghettios, ice cream and Doritos? I don't think so. But let's look at something much bigger and more important; the choices and decisions we make when dealing with problems. The choices and decisions you make should suit the situation, your age, the environment, and a host of other things. You can't solve problems the same way every time. You need to have a variety of solutions that you can sort through when different situations arise. If your cookware cabinet is limited to only a few different kinds of cookware, your choices of meals to prepare will also be limited. Likewise, your cookware cabinet of solutions should be well stocked with a variety of things to "fix" situations.

Let's say your cabinet of solutions has only one thing in it: run away. Every time a sticky situation comes up you have to consult your cabinet, but all it has in it is "run away". So, you run away every time you have to deal with a difficult situation. What good is this? This solution might work in some situations you deal with (like a skunk is coming your way), but it won't be good for too many others.

Problem solving is a delicate thing. You are faced with trying to fix situations the best way you know how, with solutions that will cause little or no damage. Sometimes you will make a bad decision, that's just life. You won't always make everyone happy with the choices you make, that's impossible. But you can't just opt to *not* make decisions for fear of making bad ones. The key is to learn from the mistakes you make and remember not to make them again. It's also a good idea to remember the good decisions you make and keep them; they are reusable! It's also a good idea to take notice of what some people do when they need to make decisions. If you have chosen good role models and mentors, you can watch how they handle some things and learn. Not all of the things they do to handle situations will work for you, however, so don't be dependent on how other people react to things as examples of how to handle your own situations. As you grow and mature you will learn better and more mature ways to solve problems, or at least that's what's supposed to happen. Some people struggle with this. If you find yourself struggling with problem solving, you're never too old to simply ask someone for help. A "Hey, what would you do if this happened to you", could save you from making a really bad decision. But like I said before, be mindful of who you choose to get advice from.

Some people never seem to break free of making bad decisions. You may know someone like this: the person who's in and out of jail, the friend that's often in trouble, that person that's always in need of someone's help because of a risk they took. I doubt you want to be this kind of person in the future, if you aren't already. Even if you've had a rocky start so far, it's not too late to turn things around.

I used to lie about stupid stuff when I was younger. Even after getting caught time after time I kept lying. I guess I was kind of hoping one day I would actually get away with a lie, it was like some crazy kind of gamble for me. Finally, it just got to be too embarrassing having to deal with the consequences, so I made a vow to myself to stop lying. Although it was very easy for me to stop, it wasn't easy for my family to believe I had. I had set up a pattern, a reputation that said I wasn't to be trusted. Sometimes I wanted to just give up and go back to lying since no one believed me anyway. But in time I gained the trust of my family, and it was a wonderful feeling! I was able to have more responsibility and knowing that I was a reliable, honest person made me feel great. And it is still an honor to know that people feel that way about me now.

A choice I made a long time ago helped me develop into the person I am today. I made that choice based on valuing how people felt about me and what kind of person I wanted to be. It took a long time to come to that decision because as a young child I didn't fully understand the importance of being honest and trusted. But as I matured, I realized you couldn't get too far without the trust of others.

So, what do you want your "decision" cookware cabinet to look like, a set of rusty undersized skillets, or one stocked with things suitable to cook gourmet meals? Even now I am still working on improving my cabinet, because opportunities to fix new meals (problems and situations) pop up all the time.

Let's Get Cookin'...

- Are you confident with the choices and decisions you make?
- How do others feel about your choices and decisions? For example, your parents, teachers, or friends... do they comment on your decision making?
- Are your decisions usually to your benefit, or do they cause you to have to work to correct them?
- Does making choices make you nervous or afraid?
- Do you often let other people make your decisions for you? And if you do, how do you feel afterwards?
- What's the hardest decision you've ever had to make? How did things turn out? What would you change about that decision if anything?
- What was the best decision you ever made? What made it good? Do you think you could use the same decision-making process over and over and achieve the same kind of results?
- What kinds of consequences have come out of your bad decisions? Was anyone else affected by those decisions?
- Who do you go to for help when making decisions? Have these people been helpful?
- Have you witnessed someone else making bad decisions, like maybe a good friend? How did it make you feel?

Caught In The Net

There was no Net when I was in junior high, not really. If I wanted to communicate with someone hundreds of miles away, I would either write a letter or get on the phone. If I wanted to find information for my research papers, it was either go to the library or surf through the encyclopedias I had at home. Now people can communicate and find info with the touch of a finger. It's awesome, yes, but it can also be pretty awful. The Net is no joke, you can find just about anything in cyberspace, yet there are many things in cyberspace that don't need to be found, especially not by a young person.

I was given a piece of advice when I was in elementary school, it was short and sweet, but powerful enough to be used for the rest of my life: don't talk to strangers. At the time this advice was given I understood that it meant if someone, particularly a male, were to approach me and try to talk to me, I was not supposed to indulge in conversation. I was supposed to get away from him quickly, and let some other adults know about it as soon as possible.

Unfortunately, nowadays it's an exciting pastime for young ladies to chat on line with men they don't know. I mean I can see how cool it might be to be able to rush home to chat with this person that tells you everything you want to hear, that makes you feel so special and thought about! You may know a guy at school you have a huge crush on and he pays you no attention at all, has no clue you exist, or makes you feel like an ugly duckling when you let him know you have this crush on him. Okay, and so having Johnny Wonderful waiting for you on line at home is just an awesome thing! But hey, Johnny Wonderful may just be a forty year old, married man with 2 children of his own that are your age. He may be a convicted child molester just released from prison, hey; he might even still be IN prison! And even if he is by some slim chance, the same age as you, his intentions may not be as honorable as he claims. His confessions of love for you are as real as unicorns, his desire to meet you and carry you away from the horrors of your everyday life with your parents or family could be your worst nightmare if you decide to take him up on his offer. If he's trying to get you to meet him and he can't come to your house, um, that's a clue right there that something's wrong. Does he give advice that is exactly what you want to hear? Guess what, that's his whole game plan, to get you to feel so safe and secure with him that you tell him everything about yourself and he will say anything in the world to make you feel like he is your number one fan. He will make you feel like everything you think and say is right and true and you think he is the Hero you've always wanted because he just makes you feel soooo special, wonderful, beautiful and cool! It's all a lie, not that you aren't wonderful, beautiful and cool, but he doesn't know you at all and only wants to take advantage of your need to feel needed, wanted and loved. He is probably telling a hundred other girls like you the same thing. Don't fall victim to his game!!!

Is he asking you to meet him secretly? Are you planning on going ahead and meeting Mr. Wonderful? Who knows about this meeting? If no one knows, you are making a huge mistake. If you've only told a friend and no adults you are headed for disaster like you've never known. I would think that when young ladies hear the stories of girls killed when they met up with some Mr. Wonderful they met online, it would keep it from happening over and over. But just like drunk drivers, some of people just don't get it! A hard head makes a soft behind, and sometimes it gets your behind in more trouble than you can get out of.

So, you've got these strangers you can meet on line, porn sites that lure you in, exciting chat rooms with all those interesting people you can't see, sites that can show you how to make a bomb, and the list goes on and on. I'm not downing the Net, like I said earlier; it can be a wonderful tool. But it can also be a gateway to things that cause your life to be changed forever in the most terrifying ways. It's not just a place that young people should be cautious, even adults need to exercise some serious caution when they are dealing with the Net.

Don't get mad when there are parental controls on the computer at your home, be glad someone cares enough to have them. If you have the chance to get your chat on with Mr. Perfect, and you refuse to understand the dangers you are placing yourself in, I don't know how many other ways I can say it: **STOP IT!** Please!

If you enjoy the thrill of doing something that feels sneaky and adventurous, try being one of the best students in your class while looking like you don't really care. Or try this one: volunteering to help the homeless and give your time and some needed help to someone that doesn't know who you are! Pretty cool huh? Yeah, there are plenty more where those came from, I challenge you to find some similar ideas.

Whatchu Lookin' At...

Are you surfing the Net without parental controls?

What kind of sites do you visit?

If you have been in a chat room who do you chat with and why?

Do you or someone you know have one of those Mr. Wonderful friends on line? If so, what kind of things does he talk about? Does it always seem like exactly the right thing?

Has he offered you something really tempting to get you to see him? If you have declined a meeting once he asked, what was his reaction? These types of people can become very threatening if they don't get what they want. They will tell you things to scare you out of letting someone know you're in contact with them. If you have found yourself in one of these online "friendships" and the guy becomes threatening, you have every right to let the police know. Tell the adult in the house, let someone know what is going on! It is entirely too easy for people to find out personal information about you just from a web address, so don't ever think you are safe because he doesn't know you; you'd be surprised what he really knows!

Am I scaring you? If so...**GOOD!** Take this seriously; people are not as nice as they sometimes make themselves appear. Here's a hint: if it feels wrong it probably is. The feeling you get when you are about to do something wrong (it could be your stomach hurting, or your heart really racing, sweaty palms...) is actually a survival instinct. That feeling is a warning that you are going to be so sorry if you do whatever it is you are thinking about. So, just DON'T do it.

Dance Lessons

One night I helped out with the youth ministry at church. When I got there, music was playing for the kids and they were all running and dancing and having a good time, just letting some time go by before the organized events began. But what I saw in that small group upset me, it made me think about my youth and what kind of dancing I did when I was their age. There were some moves I saw that came straight out of a music video. Now to see a 20 something year old woman, half naked, gyrating to the seductive and intoxicating bass rhythm of a rap artist's music is one thing. To see an 8 year old doing those same moves to a Christian rap artist's music is a whole different story. They were responding to the music and not the words. The music was very similar to a hip-hop artist's, but the words were positive, motivational and uplifting. Most of the kids weren't singing the words, they were just dancing. But when a real hip hop artist's music was played, they ALL knew the words! But did they know what the words MEANT? Nowadays it wouldn't be surprising to find that they **did** know.

I felt sort of helpless watching these children because I wasn't in charge of the event so I couldn't just stop the music and give them dance lessons and teach them how to present themselves while they had a good time dancing. What do I mean? The image of a woman, or man for that matter, dancing in a way that suggests sex, presents an image to those watching. It may make the watcher feel this person is sexually active, or that they are inviting the watcher to have sex with them. Yes, these were small children. Unfortunately, when a child's behavior does not match his or her age there are adults that are so messed up in the head that they will violate a child and say, "they wanted it" because of the way they were behaving.

So, if a little kid's dancing could set off a negative reaction and image, what happens when it is **you**? You are old enough to understand the words to the songs you sing, old enough to know what sexual intercourse is, old enough to know what images come to mind when you are bouncing your behind up and down in front of some young men or shaking your breasts in a shirt that is barely holding them. Men are very visual, that is why the pornography industry is a multibillion-dollar business. Men like to WATCH women and make a judgments about them based on how they present themselves. I speak about how your presentation of yourself affects the world that sees you in another chapter, but this is specifically dealing with imitating what you see on TV or see on the dance floor at a school dance or the skating rink (if you all still skate for fun) and how it affects or can affect your character.

When I was in elementary school, I used to love a TV show called Soul Train. I would copy what I saw on that show and was told I was a great dancer, even as a kid. When I used to watch it as a child, the dancers were all about **skill**. When the "Soul Train Line" portion of the show came on, it was about who displayed the most skill with their dancing, almost like an ice-skating competition. Years later I stopped watching it because the cameras focused on people doing moves that were seductive and vulgar, rather than graceful and skilled.

Did you know that some of the women that dance on rap videos have a life style that is dangerous, filled with promiscuity and drugs, and being passed from one man to the next like a towel? They live for the attention of the stars they dance for, but make very little money (if any), and are not respected for their dance skills but are only around to fulfill the pleasures of these men then get tossed away like a rag. Their lives revolve around things that are of no real value. Some have been strong enough to get out of the game and make better lives for themselves, while others just waste away. You can only be a video vixen so long; age and abuse will eventually put you out of the life, and then what will you do?

Maybe someone has made a comment to you about the way you dance. Maybe you have received some nasty looks from an adult that saw you gyrating and twisting to some music, or maybe you have gotten some approving stares from a group of boys, smiles or comments and it made you feel good. Let me tell you, those smiles and comments are never meant for your good, it's for their own sensory delights, and it gives them a high that can generate into a desire for you to perform those dances for them in private, without your clothes. Little things lead to bigger things. An older woman once said "A kiss is the same thing as having sex". Even though I was in my twenties, I asked, "What is she talking about?" Then I realized that she meant a kiss is just the beginning of sex, the desired end result of a romantic kiss is usually a full-blown sexual event. You could take it back even further if you want to; holding hands, looking into his eyes, a hug, a small comment, a dance move…

A coworker once laughed at me dancing and told me I needed to come out of the eighties. I told her I would never do it because some of the dancing I see now has no appeal to me and I don't want people to see me do things that don't reflect what I think and say I am: an honest, mature, self-assured woman who desires to be a role model for any young woman I come in contact with. So, think about it. Our bodies are our biggest advertising tool; we can use them for positive advertising or negative advertising. You make the choice and choose well!

Let's Dance

- How would you describe your dance style?
- Do you imitate the moves of females you may have seen on videos?
- Do the approving smiles of a young man watching you dance make you feel good? What do you think he is thinking when he sees you dancing?
- Does your dancing style reflect who you are? Or do you just do what everyone else does?
- What do you want your body to say to people and what do you do to express this?

Dead Presidents

Dead presidents, loot, cheese, ends, cash, money…it's all the same thing. How do you see it, feel about it, and plan to get it? I seem to have an "old fashioned" sense of how to gain wealth: get a job, or more than one, save, look for things worth investing in. Or there's another way, become my own boss using God given talents and knowledge I've gathered from various resources. Does this sound like a possibly slow process? Well, it could be depending on my motivation, my talents and my ideas. But it's the way I've seen my family succeed and the friends, associates and others I've spent time with.

It seems the younger generation doesn't have the same ideas about how to gain wealth. Many young people today want money the fastest way they can get it. They seem to feel it's a waste of time to get a job at a low paying workplace and try to move up. They want more material things and need a good amount of money to get them. Chances are higher for them to do things that aren't exactly honest or legal to get money. This kind of young person will make fun of the peer that works at McDonalds. They want to have on all the latest fashions, all the jewelry and "stuff" that says they are "successful" without having to do any hard work for it.

What kind of success do you desire? Do you want people to admire you for your determination, honesty and willingness to work hard for what you want? Or would you rather people be afraid of you because they don't know what you will do to get what you want: steal their car, rob their home, or even kill. There is nothing wrong with wanting to look good or have nice things. It's just that you can't do whatever you want to get those things. There is more to life than material things. And what good are material things that you acquired in a dishonest or ruthless manner when you could simply end up in jail for the way you chose to get them?

Taking the time to build wealth can be slow process. Oprah didn't become a billionaire overnight and neither did Bill Gates or other very wealthy people. But they don't have to constantly watch over their shoulders for some person they did wrong, or break out in a cold sweat if they see the police approaching them.

There was a young lady that sold drugs at a very young age. She was feared in her community and because she had something drug abusers wanted she had a power over them. They would do whatever she asked to get what she had. In turn, once she began her downward spiral and eventually had trouble with the law. It was almost impossible for her to take the advice of, listen to, trust, respect or value anything an adult or authority figure did or had to say. She felt that since she had controlled so many other adults that she could control them all and that they should all respect and fear her like her customers. She was an exceptionally talented young woman with the potential and personality to be successful in many areas. But someone in her past had told her that she was stupid; an adult, a family member. So her youth was spent trying to prove this person wrong by doing things that made her look successful, but inside she felt she was stupid and could only go so far in life. Even once she was put on the right track and had the opportunity to have a better life, she turned it down to return to her ways of attempting to have control. She ended up in jail before she was 18.

Now someone has probably made a rap song out of a story like this and instead of it emphasizing the loss of a young life due to poor choices, desire for power and negative influences, the violence and adventure of it all was probably captured and glamorized. So many young minds think it's cool to live that hard, fast kind of life themselves. They will imitate the life in as many ways as they can even if they don't actually do anything harmful. But even the imitation of this kind of life can get a person killed nowadays. If someone hears on a regular basis that the only way to get ahead is to step on the person in front of them, that life will not give them anything so they may as well take what they want, and that they will always be held back just because of where they came from or the color of their skin, they may just end up believing all this. And if they believe these things they probably won't have the desire to do things the "slow" way, and there's no telling how their story will end.

Life is a struggle at times; things may get hard for you. It may seem that it's just not worth it to be like one of the average people that goes to work and does the best they can to take care of themselves. There are many reasons why some people aren't as financially well off as others. But **everybody** isn't struggling. It's all about choices and if you make good ones, your chances of being successful are improved. If you decide you want an example to follow, be careful of the lifestyle you chose to follow. You need to know more about a person than what you might see, because all that glitters is not gold.

A Bling Thing,,,

- What is your idea of success?
- What do you think it takes to be financially secure?
- What kind of job do you want in the future? What made you choose it? What are you doing in an effort to get that kind of job?
- Do you have a plan? Do you have an image of what you would like to look like in the future?

- Is there someone encouraging you to do anything in particular? Do you like what they have to say or do you disagree?
- What person or people do you think of when you think of someone that is successful? What makes you feel that way? What do you know about this person or these people that makes you feel that they are successful? Do you know what they did to get where they are? Are you willing to do the same things?
- What kinds of things do you think would keep you from becoming successful? How do you plan to move around those obstacles?

Defending The Temple

Just for the sake of being realistic, I know that some of you are already having sex. But that does not mean that a person has the right to have you whenever they want.

One night I had a discussion with a group of young ladies. I asked some serious questions and some of the answers I got shook me pretty badly. One question I asked was: If someone (in particular someone you are supposed to be dating or in a relationship with) asks you for sex are you obligated to give it to them. Several ladies said, yes. Many of them were hesitant to raise their hands; they raised them, then thought about it and changed their minds. But one young lady insisted that she was obligated to have sex with her boyfriend if he asked, simply because he asked. I almost wasn't able to convince her that she was wrong, and it took a long discussion and the support of her peers to get her to change her view on this. This situation made me wonder how many other young women felt the same way.

There are grown women who have lost their virginity to guys that convinced them that they should have sex. Because no one ever told these women that sex was something that didn't have to be given upon request, they were robbed of being able to choose when they wanted to have their first experience. Guys will tell you just about *anything* to get you to give in to their desires. They will attempt to make you feel guilty, they will claim not getting sex causes them some physical illness. They will create a host of different reasons why they just *have* to have it. They will threaten you with the possibility of them turning to another female that *will* do it. They will tell you that you owe it to them for something that they have done for you. I could go on and on and you probably have heard some things that I didn't even mention. Sex is a **want**, not a **need**. And until you choose on your own that you want to have sex, whoever asks will just have to wait. Don't fall into that trap where a guy attempts to make you feel guilty because you had sex with someone else but aren't willing to with them. If you have already had sex and decided that you simply just don't want to do it again for a while, then that too is your choice. Anyone that tries to convince you that you have no right to hold off for a while, or forever even, is just a victim of their own weaknesses and wants you to be the same.

Anytime someone forces you to do something that is against your will, it's wrong and needs to be reported. If you have ever been forced into having sex by anyone, you need to tell someone that can help you. Regardless of how you feel, it is simply a crime and needs to be treated like one. Even if you've said yes, and then changed your mind, no is still NO, and he can't say you don't have a right to change your mind simply because he wants things to go his way! Never, ever, ever feel guilty about saying no. Once you've said it, it's a done deal and anything that happens after that is against your will. There are too many horrible incidents that have resulted from women not being taken seriously once she has said no to sexual advances. And there is no time limit to when you should let someone know what has happened to you. I know you have probably seen men that got in trouble for things they did 20 years ago. I don't suggest waiting that long, because the longer you wait the more details you forget and the harder it is to prove and the harder it is for people to believe you.

Your body is a temple, a castle, a mansion worthy of care, love and appreciation. It does not have to be shared. If someone compliments your temple it should be done in a respectful manner. But just because they gave it a compliment does not entitle them to a tour of the interior. You only get one body, you don't get to cash it in or exchange it for a better model when you get tired of the one you have. You must respect it and take care of it so that it can take care of you

Sex is something that should be shared between two mature people, able to deal with the consequences that follow. Sex should be shared between two committed (preferably married) people. Unfortunately, society has its own agenda and tends to use sex as a tool and leads people to believe that it's as right and common to do as riding a bike. Don't feel guilty if you have fallen into the trap, it's one of the hardest traps in life to avoid. But it isn't an escape-proof trap: you can leave whenever you want.

There were many days while I was working with the young ladies in my care that the subject of sexually transmitted diseases came up. Outside of possible pregnancies, this was the most common cause for stress once the girls came back from a short home visit. STDs are life crushers. Some of them are curable, while others are not. And like pregnancy, it only takes one time for it to happen. Just think, one sexual encounter that ends up changing your entire future: AIDS, herpes, genital warts...the list goes on and on. Using condoms doesn't protect you from everything, so don't even fool yourself with that one either. Many people carry STDs and don't even know it. They may have no symptoms and think all is well, telling a person they sleep with that they are healthy. They say things like, "I look healthy don't I?" Don't be fooled. Then there are those that know they have an STD and have unprotected sex anyway because they don't care if they infect someone else. Do you really want to gamble with those kinds of odds?

So, my advice of course, is to wait and choose someone you truly love and trust, preferably a spouse, before you have sex. But if you have already had the experience, you still need to really think about your future and protecting your temple. One of the worst mistakes people make when choosing to have sex is thinking that none of the bad things could possibly happen to them. Think of those trusting people who let that beautiful Trojan horse inside their gates: it was a horse of tragedy and destruction. Know that other "Trojans" can be just as dangerous!

Think about this...

- What made you choose to have sex if you already have?
- Was it totally your decision or where you talked into it?
- Did you weigh the pros and cons before you made the decision?
- Do your parents or caregivers know that you are having sex? Have you talked about it with them ever? What do they feel about it and how does it differ from your opinion, if it does?
- Do you know of anyone in your age group that has or has ever had an STD or a baby? How has it affected them?
- Has anyone every forced you into doing something sexual? Did you report it? Why or why not? What was the outcome and how do you feel about it?
- What is the "right time" to lose your virginity? What made you choose this time or date?
- Do you have a picture of what you'd like the first time to be like?
- Has a guy ever made you feel guilty for saying "no"? What were his reasons for needing it so badly? Do you feel you HAVE to say yes whenever a guy asks, if so why? If not, why?

Eyes on the Prize

I can remember one of my first real crushes. His name was Billy. I would watch him from afar and wonder if he even knew I was alive. We crossed paths every now and then but he never seemed to care much when we did. So I figured I might need to take some action in order to get his attention. Christmas was coming so I figured what could be better than for him to get a present from me! So when I was shopping for Christmas presents I picked out a nice pair of wrist bands for Billy. Wrist bands were a thing at the time; you didn't need to just wear them during sports, they become an accessory, almost like bracelets would be. So on the last day of school before break I had the wrist bands wrapped in a nice package with a little bow on top. I waited for the best time to catch Billy and walked up to him. My heart was beating so hard, I could barely breathe. I approached him and he looked at me. I said, "Merry Christmas" and handed him the gift. He tore open the wrapping paper. I was waiting to hear something like, "Oh wow, thank you!" But instead he said, "No thank you. I don't even know you." And handed them back to me.

I was crushed, and embarrassed. I couldn't really understand why he wouldn't have been overjoyed that someone had thought enough about him to get him a gift, even though he was basically a stranger. You might think this would have been lesson enough for me to not repeat the same thing. But unfortunately, some habits die hard. It was many, many years later that I realized I was wasting my time and money trying to get the attention of a guy with material things. Even when you give them something even more valuable, like your body, there is no guarantee that they will reciprocate your feelings or generosity. Seeing a guy as a prize that needs to be won is a set up for disaster in a number of ways. I realized the psychological reasons I started this behavior many years later, which is a bit too complex to go into now. But it stemmed from things that had happened to me at a very young age. I felt that if I could win the affections of a guy I liked that I could kind of fix things that had happened in my past. But like I said, it just doesn't work like that.

Have you found yourself "chasing" after a romantic interest? Do you create illusions of having some fairy tale like result for your pursuits? Do you think that if you just try hard enough or offer the right thing you will eventually get the person you want? Well, I'm here to tell you, it won't happen. You are cultivating an unhealthy characteristic within yourself. You are placing the value of whatever you choose as gifts higher than the value of yourself in whole. The fact of the matter is YOU are a priceless gift; people will either notice, and take time to develop a relationship with you, or they will not. If they choose not to, it doesn't take away from your inherent value. People create relationships with one another for an infinite amount of reasons, but it really can't be predicted who will bond with whom. You won't be able to create a bond with someone by trying to capture their will one way or another. Attempting to do so will actually only push people further away from you.

I understand that it may be very difficult at times seeing your friends or other people with a mate, partner etc. and you don't have one. You may begin to feel like something is "wrong" with you if you don't have the types of relationships you may see around you. I've mentioned throughout this book that I wasn't one of the popular or cool kids in school. I spent a lot of my time by myself or occasionally with another kid that had like interests or was genuinely nice to me. There were some kids that I could have hung out with that I chose not to simply because I didn't want to be associated with kids that were labeled as nerds, losers or nobodies by the cool kids. I was worried about what a group of kids thought that could have cared less that I was even in the building! This is just a part of growing up and being a teenager. It's a confusing and oftentimes disappointing time in our lives. You are just beginning to discover who you really are and think about who you want to become. It will take years to gain a true understanding of yourself and make better decisions about what's healthy for you in terms of relationships and romance.

In the meantime, think about some of the simple lessons that can be found in say *Cinderella* for example. She came from a sad and dysfunctional home, her friends were animals around the house, and her wardrobe was the throwbacks she got from family. But in the end, those true friends she had helped her when she really needed them, she was able to get away from the dysfunctional unhappy home and the Prince liked her without her having to chase him or offer him anything other than her friendship and true self. Use your energy to chase after your dreams for yourself rather than chase after the illusion of romance and happily ever after. You will have the best relationships when you are sure of your love for yourself and know that you create your own happiness, it's not a prize to be sought after.

And the Winner is…
- Is there someone you have a crush on that you are devoting time and energy in effort to get their attention? If so, what made you choose this person?
- Does this person return your affections/attention?
- If they don't do you try harder? Do you criticize yourself for not being able to get them to like you?

- The time (or money) you are spending on this person, could you find a better way to use it? Consider this; who would benefit more from your time and efforts and possibly give you a sense of appreciation in return?

If you are comparing yourself to others you will never be happy. Your path is your own and trying to make it match someone else's is a terrible waste of time. Sometimes you have to "date yourself" meaning, you give yourself that time and effort you would give someone you really like. When you appreciate and care for yourself, it reflects in everything else you do and you might find that you end up drawing good healthy friends into your world. That's where a healthy romantic relationship should start.

Fashion Police

How you dress can be an expression of what you feel inside. You may or may not be able to dictate what you wear. I wasn't able to pick my own clothes for school until I was almost out of high school! I might choose an outfit to wear and my aunt would tell me to go change. Sometimes you are being told to change for reasons that make sense (too tight, too revealing, too wrinkled). Other times it's just the personal feelings of your parents or guardians. This can be one of the most difficult issues for teens. You want to express your sense of independence, show the world who you are so to speak, by the way you dress. The way you present yourself is important. So if you have a lot of control over your choices I suggest you choose wisely; be it what you wear, or how you style your hair, do it with care.

I didn't have much say in what I got to wear to school. My clothes were picked out at the beginning of the school year by my family. If I wore something they didn't approve of I was told to go change before I left the house. Yes, I was highly upset when this happened but they had their reasons for objecting and so I had to deal with it. There was one time I was able to make it to school in some jeans I'd turned inside out. There was a rap duo at the time that wore their clothes inside out and or backward, so of course kids were imitating their styles. Well, I didn't make it past the front hallway at school. Our security guard saw me, and just pointed and said, "No." So I had to turn them right side out, and that was that.

If you have control over your fashion choices, you have to be aware of what you are saying to the world when you step out of the house. As much as I love to see how creative teens are with their fashion expressions, there are times when I am saddened by how offensive some of their choices can be.

Wearing clothes that are too tight is both unattractive and unhealthy. If your stomach is showing because your shirt is too small or you have chosen one that is supposed to show your stomach, why do you think this is okay for school? If your underwear is showing, why? It's called UNDERwear for a reason. Victoria's Secrets... *SECRETS*, get it?

Wearing pants that are too tight restricts the airflow and circulation to your body. If you have ever had a yeast infection you know how bad it itches and how bad it smells! If you wear tight pants, you increase the chances of having one as well as other bacterial and fungal infections. Your vagina needs to breathe. If it can't, it will hold in things that need to come out and it creates the conditions for an infection. If you can't move freely in the outfit you are wearing, why wear it?

Now that the ideals for what is acceptable in society have slackened, and decreased it affects the way we dress in a number of environments. Who knew it would ever be ok to wear pajamas outside, to the mall, or to the grocery store!? With this lowering of standards comes the unfortunate issue of having to see people dressed inappropriately.

Your fashion choices can reflect good things about you, and bad things about you. You don't have to dress in things that reveal more about you than they should in order to gain the approval of others. There is a sense of rebellion that comes with being a teenager, I get it. But, taking pride in your appearance is more important than making a stand for your independence. You can make fashion choices that express your personality, without being half naked or inappropriate. You can also dress fashionably without having to spend a lot of money for your clothes. People will put a name on you simply by how you present yourself, without ever saying a word to you or being introduced to you. People tend to judge a book by its cover. If the cover is tastefully done and looks valuable they will see it that way. But a book without a cover is pretty much worthless; it looks like it's missing something, vulnerable, trash. It won't be treated with the respect that the one with a nice cover gets.

My point is, consider what you want to say to the world when you get dressed each day. Consider what your parents or guardians had to do to get what you are wearing. Consider what you expect to experience from the world when they see you coming. If you are dressed respectfully, you will probably get treated more respectfully. If you are dressed in a way that shows the world more than it needs to see, that can be taken in a number of ways, but it won't always be positive. What you have under your clothes is for your eyes only, it shouldn't be busting loose from your clothes. Your clothes shouldn't constrict your breathing, cause pain, cut off your circulation, distract or prevent you from doing things that are important, like walking, reaching and bending over...breathing.

You may not like the fashion police, but they are there to serve and protect.

You have the right to remain respectful...

- If you have freedom to choose your fashions have you ever had a problem for instance being in trouble at school for what you chose to wear? Or has an adult ever commented about your outfit in a negative way?
- What do you want to say to the world when you choose an outfit? What do you want the world to say about you?
- Have you ever been complimented for an outfit? Who gave the compliment and how did it make you feel?
- Have you ever looked at your classmates and criticized what they were wearing? What made you disapprove?

On the opposite...what has someone wore that you really liked and why?

Filling The Gaps

Now I know that not every reader believes in God, but I do and so I feel I would be shorting myself and you if I didn't express how my faith has helped mold me into the person I am today. Perhaps my sharing this will give someone else the motivation to seek God in his or her own lives. It would be awesome if someone were moved to change the way they felt about the existence of a Supreme Being, God, or Creator etc. But I've learned to not attempt to push people into agreeing with me about this. It's ultimately your own decision what you choose to believe, so I'm just asking that you take the time to read what I have to say rather than flip to the next chapter because you don't want to be "preached to." No preaching, I promise, just perspective.

I wasn't always one to talk about my faith, or attempt to get people to examine his or her own. The only time I went to church when I was growing up was when family took me if I spent the weekend at their homes. I didn't enjoy it because I never had the right clothes to wear. Since I wasn't a regular, my wardrobe was light on nice things to wear like dresses and such. By the time I wore the dresses I had, they were too small or out of date. I felt awkward being around the other teens that were always dressed so nicely. I also felt uncomfortable because I didn't know the other kids. I felt like an outsider and knew I'd never get a chance to know them because I wouldn't be back at church for a few weeks or even months. It wasn't until my second year of college that I started going to church on a regular basis and began my journey of learning about God. By then I had gotten into so many unhealthy habits that it was extremely difficult to break away from them. Over the years I drifted farther away from the thing I needed most: a connection to God and a life centered on things He was trying to teach me.

I was used to asking God for things when I needed them, praying pretty regularly and blessing my food. Sometimes I talked to Him more and felt close to Him, and other times I wondered where He was. One period in my life I was having a really hard time. I didn't know what to do and felt every decision I made was only making my hole deeper. Then someone suggested I write a letter to God. I figured I had nothing to lose so I did it, very specific, detailed and heartfelt. I was completely drained after I finished, so I went to bed. The next day, everything that was wrong, was right. God sent people that helped me, a clearer mind to think about certain decisions, and basically put everything in line. By the next night I could go to sleep without tossing and turning wondering what I should do next. I was so grateful that I made a promise to go to Him for everything, to pray before I made any significant decisions, to allow myself to learn about Him and listen to Him, and to act like I had some sense instead of just doing whatever I wanted and suffering the consequences later. I discovered that God was really always near and actually listens to me and provided things for me when I needed them. I may not have gotten things when I felt I should, but when I did get them I often realized it was right on time. Which meant I could trust God. This was more than I could say for most of the people in my life.

There are many faiths out there, and just as many people doing what they can to influence others to be a part of their faith. I had to follow my heart, and be open-minded. The times I've spent involved in worship at a number of different churches and places of worship have come to shape a part of how I feel about God and the way I need to live my life. It was difficult to find places that had what I needed sometimes. I've moved a lot in my life so there weren't always the kinds of churches in the areas I lived in that fit what I felt I needed. So I found other ways to learn and experience worship. I watched pod casts on the internet or found programs on TV that were just as resourceful as being in an actual sanctuary. Your journey will be your own. If you allow yourself to listen to your inner voice and listen to people who give you good advice, in time you will know what's best for you in terms of how you see God and experience Him in your life.

Honestly, how you decide to practice your faith will be molded over the years as you grow into learning about yourself and life. I guess I'm asking that you consider your faith if you haven't and take the time to begin learning about God and His love for you.

God gave me the idea to write this book with the intent of sharing wisdom and experiences that might positively guide young women through those trying and difficult teenage years. Without Him and the encouragement of friends and people that have a real interest in me, this book would just be a wish floating around inside me.

This is a complex subject. One's faith is something like a building; it starts with a plan and is built over time. As the years go by the building may need renovations, upgrades, improvements and necessary changes or additions. And sadly some people completely demolish their buildings because of things that have happened to them or that they've seen happen to others. They may choose to rebuild, but it may take time. When they listen to their hearts they'll know what to do.

I can say this with the most confidence though, prayer is the fastest way to get God's attention! Prayer is simply talking to God. He wants you to talk to him, he made you for that reason, to communicate with him. Even if you feel like you don't know what to say, just start with something as simple as, "God I thank you for today, yesterday and tomorrow". He's a friend, so treat him like it and talk to him like you would any trusted love one. You may even get mad at Him sometimes, it's a part of any relationship you have. But He won't be mad at you for being honest. His desire is that you come to Him and give Him the opportunity to show you His love so you can trust Him. Spend time with him; He's always there. I can only say these things because I've experienced them and it would be a shame if I didn't share how God has impacted my life. My prayer is that you are able to feel the awesomeness of His love in your life as soon as you can rather than later.

What next...
- Does your family go to church? Do you go when and if they do?
- Do you have a curiosity about God?
- Have you tried to get answers about things dealing with God and just felt lost when listening to what others have to say?
- Do you feel like something is missing in your life that no **person** can fill?
- What do you think church should be like? If you have been in the past, what things did you enjoy? What things did you dislike?
- What is your image of God? What do you know about Him and where did you learn it?
- What kind of things do you expect to have when you believe in God?
- What kind of life do you want to lead and how do you feel your faith or lack thereof will shape your life?

I am using the work God from my own experiences. There are many terms for this: God, Creator, the University, I Am, Lord…and many more. As I've said, God is all around, not just to be found at a church. My hope is that you consider how you feel about Creation in general and a higher power that gives you a sense of connection with this world like no other. There will be people that don't believe in God (or any of the other terms), and that is a matter of choice. Something I've learned that's been very important to me is to respect what others believe even if you don't believe the same. Listening to other people's feelings about their faith allows you to learn about them and the world. As you listen to others and have your own experiences, you will generate your own feelings about your faith.

Guiding Light

Everyone one of us has an inner voice. It has a number of different names: conscience, common sense, intuition, the Holy Spirit, gut feeling, and that "thing" inside. I think it works differently for each person. For me, the feeling or voice goes with the situation; at times, it's a quiet reassuring voice, other times it's a loud voice of warning. Other times, it's an urging to push forward, and it can be a pulling to sit still and be quiet. This guide within us was placed there for a reason, to keep us alive, out of harm's way, to keep us from hurting ourselves and hurting others.

Now, the thing about this little gift we all have is the way we chose to use it. I don't always listen to my little voice. Sometimes I let my stubborn self shout down my little voice. If I see a really nice pair of shoes that I may not have the money for, my little voice may say, "Sonja, not now", but my stubborn self may say "whatever" and I go ahead and get them. However, it's not too long after making a decision against my little voice that I come to regret the decision I made and I'm left sitting somewhere saying, "I knew I shouldn't have done that!"

Sometimes the damage done when you don't listen to your guide is minimal. You can take back that outfit you bought if you haven't already worn it and gotten make up on it. On the other hand, sometimes the damage is enormous; you could hurt people, hurt yourself, or worse.

Some people learn from their pasts. They recognize times when they didn't listen to their guide and they try harder to follow it. Then there are those that just refuse to listen and continue to make the same mistakes over and over, no matter what their friends say, their parents, anyone, they just have to do it on their own.

I discovered that the more I did things my way, the more chaotic my life became. I had no control over anything. I was lost and ended up trying to fix the things I had broken. Unfortunately, I've spent too much of my time feeling like a gerbil on a wheel running and running to get someplace and all the while I stayed in the same spot.

When I was in college I racked up a number of credit cards. College students are like test mice to bankers and financial institutions. They know they can pretty much lure them into making some big commitments that they will end up paying for long after they are finished with school, if they even get to graduate. Credit companies put out a little cheese and watch the mice come scrambling to it. There were credit card brochures all over the place. You know, when you want something and someone is telling you, "Hey, you can have this now and just pay a little every month", you say," Hmmm...that's not a bad idea". However, if you don't take time to read the fine print you won't see that there's more to it than that. If you borrow money from any institution or company, you don't just pay back what you borrowed. There's this thing called interest. Interest is a percentage of the total amount you borrowed, and there's a monthly percentage that is added to your total balance. Say for instance you borrow $100 from the bank, at an interest rate of 20%. You plan on taking your time paying it back, but you didn't think about the interest rate, which will be $20. So every month 20% of your balance will be added on to what you already owe. To make this extra tempting, the bank will send you a bill and it will say you only need to pay $2 towards that bill. You're like great, this is cool and take your sweet time paying it off. But you are forgetting that by the time you pay the bill off, you may have paid well over $200, due to the interest charges that piled up.

Now that I've finished my financial lesson...I got one card after another, had several balances on each one, paying the little bit each month that the bill required. I later realized I was paying $20 to each of these cards and my balances weren't going down! It was because each card had an interest rate of over 20%! There was no way I could get them paid off paying the little bit they were asking for, plus I was still using them making the balances even higher! Now, once I realized this it took a long time to get it under control. By this time, it was a habit. I would pay off one card but lose my mind because there was a zero balance and go and use it again! Once I got all of them paid off with the help of advisors and personal discipline, I got crazy again and repeated the cycle. But, you know once I took a look at my credit report, and saw how much money I had wasted over the years I was devastated. I could have had the house of my dreams and the car, too, if I'd been more disciplined with my money. By the way, a credit report is a record of all the places you paid bills to and a record of whether you did it on time. It is one of the most import things in each of our lives. I suggest you have your parents or even someone at the bank explain how credit works and how banking services work. If you don't know how to control your money, it will definitely control you and that is an awful way of life.

What's this got to do with my inner guide? I didn't LISTEN to it! Every time I filled out a new credit application my "gut" was telling me, "Sonja, you might not want to do this". But I just wanted to have those new Nikes, that sundress, those dishes, that car, that furniture. I wanted it all right then even though I knew I would be feeling it in a really bad way later if I didn't have the money to pay those bills on time. I went on the hopes that I would have something in the future, but didn't make choices thinking about what my money looked like at that very moment.

I've paid emotionally when I didn't listen to my guide when it came to relationships too. Not just relationships with guys, but with my family, coworkers, and people I've met over the years. Emotional costs are worse than financial ones many times, because you can fix the financial ones, but you can't always fix the emotional ones. Pain and hurt caused by someone or even caused by yourself is a monstrous thing to defeat if you don't know how to accept your part in situations. Try to listen to both sides of an argument, forgive, and seek help when it's beyond your ability to repair. Without God in my life, none of my pains or hurts would be healed right now. Without a relationship with God I would still be a mess, financially and emotionally. He's always there, even on bank holidays. Also God has sent me a lot of smart, financially responsible people throughout my life that have taught me things and given me wisdom and advice. I didn't always listen to them, but I never forgot what they told me. And when I did follow their advice and saw how it worked I thanked them and made a promise to share what I learned...like I'm trying to do now!

So, your inner guide is an all- purpose guide. It tells you about people, risky situations, the weather, money, your health, how to wear your hair, whether your decisions are good or bad, when to do your homework, and even what time to go to bed. It's there for you always, but it's up to you to use it wisely!

Step Into the Light:
- Have you ever heard or felt your inner voice?
- When you experienced it, what did you chose to do? Did you listen to it, or push it to the back of your mind?
- Have you felt the consequences of not listening to the guide? What happened?
- Have you felt the rewards of listening to it? What happened?
- Do you find it difficult to listen to yourself and trust in your common sense? Has anyone ever accused you of not having any common sense? If you've had a problem in this area, are you doing anything to try to improve?

Handle Your Business

Even though I grew up with people that had entrepreneurial spirit (the desire to own their own businesses), it didn't really seep into my personality. I was talented in many ways as a child but wasn't sure how I could find ways to make a career out of those talents. I was a decent artist, a gifted reader, and had a wonderful imagination and creativity. But, I was more into giving away my works of art to get people to like me than thinking about using my talents to create a lasting source of income.

I got my first job as a community newspaper deliverer when I was in junior high. It was an all right job but it was not a paper that required payment; payment was voluntary. Regardless of the fact that I delivered the papers all by myself faithfully when they arrived in stacks at my house, my income would only increase if I was able to get people to volunteer to pay. Selling things was not a strength of mine; I didn't like having to ask or convince people to buy things. I wasn't a sales person at heart, especially not with the product I was working with.

When I got to college and had more freedom to explore options for income, I kept remembering this guest speaker that had come to my high school. He told us that we needed to take an active role in securing a future that was financially secure. He talked about how he found a way to make money by recovering undamaged bricks from demolition sites and taking them to construction companies. His business grew tremendously and he became a very lucrative businessman. So with his speech echoing in my mind, I decided to take my financial future into my own hands. I created a flyer that let people know I was available to help with chores around their homes. I made lots of copies and went into the neighborhood near my school. I put the flyers on doors until I ran out of them. It took a few days but I finally got a call. It was from an older woman that lived alone and needed help with some things at her house. I was excited. I went to meet her, she seemed pleasant and the house was very large, so I felt needed. I did yard work, windows, swept sidewalks, whatever she could come up with. But the problem was that I didn't know what to charge her once I was done. I would just tell her to give me whatever she felt it was worth. I worked for her for a little while but felt the need to make more money. So I found a job working at a very chic clothing boutique. That job was pretty nice but the owner wasn't very honest so I had to move on. I also wanted to be more in control of what I did so that it was as close to being something I was doing for myself rather than someone else.

One of my proudest moments was when I answered a request for writers in the paper. There was a man looking to start a new magazine and I definitely wanted to be a part of that. All I had to do was write the articles for the subjects he provided. I did, and seeing my article appear in a real magazine was the most awesome thrill. But the money thing once again became an issue. I told them what I wanted to be paid for the article and they gave me the run around. Because I was an amateur writer, I wasn't sure what my work was worth. I had to call one of my professors to get help, and eventually I got paid the amount I'd asked for. As I write this I can only imagine the thrill I'll get seeing the finished project on the shelves of a bookstore!

So, what's my point you ask? It's that if you have a talent, use it! This is the day of the home businessman/ businesswoman. Thousands of people have seen the advantages to being able to work out of their homes and make more money than when they were working for someone else. Home business owners and small business owners are to be admired. They are willing to start their businesses from a dream they've had, suffer the consequences involved, face the possibility of losses (financial and otherwise), and take control of their financial futures.

Everyone has some talent at something. It's a shame that many people don't realize that they have the potential to market their skills. They let other people talk them out of starting their own businesses because they think it's too hard. Have you ever heard of the Crab Barrel mentality? It's like this: crabs in a barrel will pull each other down trying to get out of the barrel. They don't care who it may hurt, just so long as that other crab doesn't get out before they do. Some people have crab barrel mentality; they will do and say all they can to keep someone they associate with from achieving more than they do. They'll come up with every negative thing that "could" happen and the person with the dream gets cold feet and may never even make an attempt.

I am always impressed with people that start small businesses that eventually expand. And most of these people started out doing things in their homes; making bread, experimenting with a design, finding a better way to do something. I know some young women who are extremely talented hair stylists and they charge a very small amount compared to women in salons that aren't nearly as good. Sometimes you will need some education and certifications to get your business going. If you can get it, then do it, it will be a huge advantage in the future. If you can get the education for free that's even better. I didn't take advantage of the vocational department of my high school because I didn't understand it! I didn't see then that if I learned a trade skill I would be marketable as soon as I graduated from high school. I learned recently that because high schoolers don't understand the benefits of trade school or have a low opinion of them based on things they hear and see in our current social attitudes, that the US is critically short of tradesmen and tradeswoman. What that means is the people that fix your air conditioning and heat at home, or your car, or fix things in your house that break (walls, plumbing, roofing) that there are much longer wait times for these repairs to be done and people have to pay more for them since there are fewer people to call for help!

Take time to explore your talents, then, think about your future, and especially your financial stability. Don't allow your family's circumstances to be the blueprint for your future; meaning, just because your family may not live in the suburbs or have lots of money doesn't mean that you can't one day live in a nice neighborhood or even become a millionaire. Don't allow yourself to be brainwashed into believing that you do not deserve to have the best for yourself and financial stability and security. You are entitled to doing the best you can for yourself. Never be ashamed to dream big and never feel guilty when your dreams do come true. There is always room at the top.

Business Sense
- Is there something you do that has other people coming to you for favors and requests? How often do you ask for something in return if you do the favor or request? Note: it's nice to be nice, giving people things is fine most of the time. The saying that it's better to give than receive is all right for a time, but there's also a time when it's strictly business. I could have opened a gallery with all the pictures I've drawn for people and I don't have anything to show for it now. I could have at least made copies and kept the originals!

- Are you trusted to do something that other young women your age are not? Like for example; baby sit, walk a dog, watch someone's house while they are away, make meals or desserts, create a specific craft, etc? Have you been paid for these things?

- Are you a naturally outgoing person? Are you bold when speaking and letting others know that you have ideas that may be worthwhile?
- Do you have a savings account? If so, what kind of things are you saving for?
- If not, why not?
- When you see someone that is "rich" can you imagine that being YOU? Do you believe it's possible or do you think it just can't happen? What do you think it takes to become rich or financially secure?

Suggested reading: autobiographies of Madame C.J. Walker, Benjamin Franklin, George Washington Carver.

Other research stuff: take time to skim through some finance magazines and see what kind of ideas people have come up with that have led them to become very successful business people. If you know someone that owns their own business, ask them how they got started. Most of them will be more than willing to give you their story and you may be surprised to learn about their lives, they didn't all start out in the best of circumstances!

Hills, Valleys and Depressions

Females get talked about pretty badly at times because we show our feelings. I don't know how many times I've heard people comment on the way females cry easily. I cry easily; I cry when I'm really happy, when I'm sad, when I get mad, at weddings and funerals. Did you know that all these tears are all very different? Depending on the emotion that caused the tears, their chemical composition will be different. I think that's pretty cool! But this isn't all about crying. There are sooo many emotions, and females seem to be able to experience them all and sometimes even within a single day! Contrary to what some people say, this is not always a bad thing. You can be a very emotional person and still be functional and productive. It's when you cannot control these emotions that you may have some serious problems.

Picture this; your emotions are sort of like hills, valleys and depressions. When you are feeling high, happy, and great, you're in the hills. When things are going just fine and no drama or extra pressures are present you could say you are in the valley. Then there are the depressions, the low points and the pits. Each one of us journeys through all these landscapes, but we journey through them differently. Some people stay in the hills more than the valleys, some stay in the depressions more than the hills. It all depends on how we handle our lives, deal with stress and solve problems. It also depends on our environment. You may live in a household that isn't very happy, lots of stress and unhappiness and you may find it very difficult to find valleys or hills. You may not even know that you don't have to always be in the depressions and that there are ways to get out. Some people get so used to being in the depressions that it becomes a way of life. These people can't handle being joyful because they feel it won't last anyway and things are bound to make a turn for the worse. I can't handle being around people like this! They are capable of pulling others down into the pits with them. I know because I used to be one of those people. Then someone told me how much of a drag I was and I started getting my act together. Now I do all I can to have fun, not to be so serious about everything and laugh as much as possible. I feel physically lighter when I am happy and people are nicer to me when they see me happy.

No, you can't always expect things to work out the way you want them to. You are going to have rough times and then some great times. You know, it's not the situation that changes your attitude; it's how your attitude can change a situation. Let's say, when you got up to get ready for school you realized your little brother had used your lip gloss to do a coloring project. It was your favorite lip gloss. You get really angry, but there's nothing you can do about it. You have some choices though, as far as your attitude. You could go to school and take it out on everyone, yell at your little brother and make him feel bad, go through the entire day a big sour puss, or simply understand that he's just a kid, and you can get another lip gloss later. When you dictate your attitude, no situation should be able to change it. People may say, "Oh! She made me so mad!" Really, it's that they allowed someone to change their mood. No one can control your moods. They can attempt to, but it's not possible. You have complete control over them, it's mind over matter; if you don't mind, the situation doesn't matter.

If you feel like you truly cannot control your emotions, no matter how much you try, you might want to consider talking to someone about this. Let someone know your concerns. Sometimes you don't realize how much your moods are changing, you think it's just a regular thing to go from screaming mad to calm as a cucumber in a matter of seconds. However, if your moods are causing you problems, you need to find some help. Talk about it with your family, the school nurse, your guidance counselor, someone at church, the family doctor…you don't have to let your moods control your life.

There are lots of companies out there trying to take advantage of people's struggles with their emotions. They offer a host of different medications to help people feel better. Yes, some people need medication to help control emotional issues, but there are some who are so desperate to feel better that they think the medication will be the best bet without looking at other options. I am an advocate for talking about things, getting them off my chest and finding ways to get rid of problems naturally without having to risk drug side effects and whatnot.

I used to work at the post office. It was an extremely stressful environment for me, and on top of that, I was going through some personal issues. One day a woman that worked there, who people said was standoffish and not very nice, came up to me and told me something that I will never forget. She said, "Never be afraid to talk to someone about your problems. Don't ever be ashamed to get counseling. It saved my life." She gave me a brief history of her life when things were at their worse and how her decision to seek help saved her from continued misery. I felt God was sending me a message through her. I love it when someone has dealt with a situation similar to mine and can give me first hand advice. It's one of the reasons I am writing this book now, so you can see that I am not just telling you how to deal with some of life's situations, but to let you know how I was able to get through some of them myself. You never know who may be able to listen to you and help just by listening. So don't be afraid to talk with someone about what's happening with you.

Sometimes just hearing yourself discuss a problem allows you to come up with solutions without you having to hear advice from the person with whom you are talking.

So where are you headed and where do you want to spend most of your time emotionally: hills, valleys, or depressions?

Where are you?
- Where do you spend most of your time: hills, valleys, or depressions, and why?
- What is the general attitude you have most of the time? What directly affects your attitude each day, (examples: your friends, your family, school, the weather)?
- How do people, especially strangers, respond to you most of the time?
- Do you like the landscape that you spend your time in? If not, what do you think you can do to change it?
- Take some time to think about how certain environments affect your mood. Once you've come up with some, think about why that environment causes the feeling it does. Then try this experiment: go into that environment and concentrate on trying to feel something different. Taking time to learn why you feel a certain way at a certain time is important. The more you understand you feelings, the more you are able to control them.

I'm Every Woman

What does it take to become a woman? You could probably get a number of different answers from a number of different people. But the one thing that comes to my mind is when you start your menstrual cycle. Don't get me wrong now. I don't think you are instantly a woman once you get your period, it's just that some people relate the ability to have a baby with the onset of womanhood.

How much do you know about your body? Do you know what a menstrual cycle is? Do you know why you have one? What kinds of things have you heard about it? Of all the things you know, how much is fact, and how much is fiction?

I heard so many different things before and at the onset of my cycle that I wasn't sure what to think. I didn't know whether to be scared or happy when it came. I was lost basically. My family didn't prepare me for this change in my life and I didn't feel comfortable going to them for information. I remember I had to bring home a permission slip one day because my middle school was having a whole day dedicated to sex education. I wasn't sure if my aunt would sign it or not. I was scared to even give it to her. Even after I gave it to her and she signed it, I wasn't sure if she had really read it and understood what it was asking. I felt like I was doing something sneaky and secret even though she'd given me permission. When the day finally came at school we watched a lot of movies and had some discussions. My teachers were dedicated to answering any questions we had and giving us a clear understanding of the information so we wouldn't walk away confused, embarrassed, scared or ashamed. Nevertheless, I was still all of those things because I didn't ask any questions when I had the chance. I wasn't sure what to ask. Besides I didn't want to talk to my teachers about that kind of stuff, I wanted to talk to someone I knew a lot better on a more personal level.

Before I get too far into this, let me give as simple an explanation of the menstrual cycle as I can. Every female has some basic reproductive organs: a uterus, two fallopian tubes and two ovaries and a vagina. At birth a female's ovaries have eggs already produced and being held inside. At a certain point in her life, usually between the age of 9 and 15 her body knows that it's time to allow the eggs to be released. The egg is being released so that it can possibly become fertilized and become a life; a baby. Before the egg is released the uterus prepares itself for the egg. The inside of the uterus gets thick and filled with extra blood and tissue to support an egg should it become fertilized. The egg will come down from the ovaries, through one of the fallopian tubes and settle in the uterus until it is either fertilized or flushed away. If the egg is not fertilized, the lining of the uterus sheds and comes out of the vagina: that's why you bleed. If the egg is fertilized it begins developing and growing inside the uterus, becoming a baby. The most common way for an egg to be fertilized is from having sex and the sperm from the male travels up through the vagina, into the uterus, finding a waiting egg.

That explained, having a menstrual cycle is nothing to be ashamed of! It is a normal part of life. You should never feel like it's something nasty or dirty. Guys that don't have a clue about how a female's body works tend to act a fool even at the mention of a period. They will make stupid, insensitive, rude and mean comments about the subject just to try to make you feel bad. Whatever they say, just pay it no mind. Being a female is a wonderful thing, even if there are times when you wonder why you have to go through so much!

One of the best things I did for myself when I was younger and wanted to know something, was to read about it. I still read as much as I can about health matters. I want to be as knowledgeable about my body as I can. I would always get upset when I had to go to the doctor's office and they would ask me when my last menstrual cycle was, I could never remember! If I didn't write it down I wouldn't be able to answer them and I would just make up a date as close to it as I could. I never took the time to count the days between cycles. I admired females that could tell exactly when they had had their last period. It wasn't until recently that I actually counted the days and realized that every 28 days I had a cycle. That explained why some months I would come on twice. Of all the information I knew about herbal remedies and how to kill a cold, I'm a bit ashamed to have just figured out that simple information about my body.

I'm not sure how schools are handling this issue anymore; if they are having whole days dedicated to informing students about their reproductive systems or how much info they are providing in science classes. But don't just leave it in the hands of your teachers to give you information. If your family hasn't told you things you feel you need to know, then ask them. If they for some reason can't help you then try to find someone that can give you accurate information: a teacher, nurse, doctor another female in your family whom you trust and feel confident will give you good info. **Never guess**, make up stuff, or assume you know things about something as serious as this. I got a lot of information when I did finally get my period but none of it was very good. None of it helped me when I wasn't feeling good and had to stay home from school. Some females have a very hard time with their menstrual cycles and some barely notice they have one. Partly this is due to genetics; many of the women in my family had problems. So get some family history if you can. If I had taken the time to discover information about how the body works I would have been able to avoid some of the discomforts and embarrassing situations I've experienced. Your body will actually tell you what it needs. If you pay attention to your cravings and how your diet affects your body you too can avoid some headaches in the future.

My family did not discuss the things I needed to know about my body. I was very afraid to even bring it up. The one time I did the experience was uncomfortable enough that I knew I'd never do it again. You may have to feel out your family, see who you think will talk to you honestly and openly. It is unfortunate when you have to go outside your family to get help, but it's worth it to be as prepared as possible, even if you have to do the research on you own.

You will have plenty of decisions to make when your time comes. Many things are trial and error. What works for one person doesn't always work for someone else. Love your body enough to take the time to find out what it needs and what is best for it. It can be really confusing and scary going through this time in your life when you don't have very much information about it. And keep in mind that you continue to learn as you grow. Becoming a woman is a process, but a beautiful one none the less.

What you know now...
- Have you had the chance to be educated on your body and things that are supposed to happen with it as you mature?
- If you are clueless about menstruation and changes your body is going through is there anyone you feel comfortable talking to that's an adult?

- Who have you spoken to about some of your concerns? Do you feel embarrassed to bring up the subject and if so, why?

- Was there a day dedicated to this info at your school? Is the subject introduced in Health Class? If it was, did you ask any questions? If not, did you wish you had later?

- Do your friends discuss any of the things your bodies are going through and attempt to find out why if you don't know? If your friends are comfortable talking about it, make a point to get good information and not just guess and listen to the myths.

- If you are already experiencing have a cycle, how are you handling it? Are you comfortable dealing with it or are there things you'd like to be able to change? Do you talk with your friends about their experiences and how they handle their cycles?

I think it's very empowering to learn as much as you can about your body. When you can understand why certain things happen it's easier to know how to change or improve things. I learned in my 20s that my diet was a factor in why my cycles were so bad. I changed my diet and my cycles were not nearly as bad. Over the years I've had to make modifications to my diet in order to help my body work better and manage my cycles when they became difficult. Pay attention to your body and how certain things like diet and exercise affect you.

Is It In You?

My sister was aggravated with my nephew one day because she'd gotten in his car for something and when she started it up some rap music came blaring out of the speakers. Now this would have been fine if it had been Christian rap, but it was filled with obscenities and sexual content. When she confronted my nephew, he told her that the CD was not his, he had borrowed it. This made the situation worse because he knew that he wasn't allowed to listen to that kind of music. At first I didn't understand what the big deal was because at the time my music collection had some questionable stuff in it. When I asked my sister why she was so angry she explained that the music you listen to becomes a part of you. She said that if you listen to music that's full of curse words and sex you will sooner or later live what you listen to: you will allow curse words to be a part of your vocabulary and your values towards sex may end up matching those of the music. Then I got it. I always wondered why some females allowed themselves to be called "bitch" and "ho", it drove me nuts! Then I watched some of the videos on the music channels and really listened to the words in some of the songs and understood that they were living what they listened to and what they watched on T.V. I was disturbed. It's not that the videos and the music were new to me, or that I'd just realized how the material affects impressionable young minds. Once it hit close to home, I realized my lifestyle needed some adjustments. I knew I had allowed my nephews to listen to my music when we were together and I felt awful that I may have contributed to the destruction of their morals.

Yet it goes deeper than just music; it's movies, books, television shows, games, and lots of other things that we feed our minds with. It's called *entertainment* for the most part, but when you really look at what some people find entertaining, it's kind of scary at times.

There's a huge debate about whether video games that contain lots of violence lead people to act out violently. Some people say that when you play the violent video games that you are releasing tensions and doing it in a harmless way, by using the images on a screen. People against the games say that playing the games will cause you to be less sensitive to real violence and more and more people will see violence as just an everyday part of life. With the increase in hostile and violent behavior, witnessed from daily news, you have to consider the possible truth to what has been said about the negative effects of these games. Also, what's on TV now is really different than in the past. Words that were once forbidden to be used are commonly used now. Scenes of sex and violence are common as well sadly. People seem to be so desensitized that they don't see anything wrong with using profanity in public, any time and any place. And the same seems to be true with guns and violence.

I decided that I needed to do some revision in areas of my life, as far as what I did for entertainment. I ended up getting rid of a lot of CDs and making very different decisions when I rented movies or watched them at the theater, even what I listened to on the radio. I found that my language changed, as well as the conversations I had and the kind of people I chose to spend my time with. Some people might find this extreme or too much to handle. They don't want to give up their habits, or change a few friends. Personally, I don't regret a thing because I know I live a lifestyle that carries much less stress. I don't have to worry that something I do might negatively influence a child, or a teenager, for that matter. If there are young people around me and I feel uncomfortable about something I'm doing, I have to think, is it something I really need to be doing at all, whether they are around me or not.

So, what's in you? What do you allow to fill your imagination, your spare time, your world? It's sort of like that saying, "you are what you eat"; if you eat lots of junk food, you're probably not a very healthy individual and your outside appearance will surely reflect what kind of diet you have. So if the things you entertain yourself with are filled with unhealthy things (violence, sexual content, drug use, videos with females dressing with little to nothing, music expressing hate and anger), eventually your outside appearance and behaviors will reflect those things too. Even if you don't see yourself as a role model and don't want to be one, the things you do can still influence someone else. I don't know about you, but I don't ever want to be the one that leads someone else down the wrong path.

Nope, not talking about Gatorade...
- What do you do with your spare time? What's your entertainment?
- Have you ever had to keep a younger child away from something you were doing because you were afraid of how it might affect him or her?
- Have you ever had someone imitate something you normally do and felt embarrassed by the imitation? An example of this is how kids copy something they've seen someone else do. They usually end up getting in trouble for it and it's not really their fault if they had no idea what they were imitating.
- Do you act out some of the things you do for entertainment? For instance, do you copy the dances you see on videos, reenact fight scenes or sing lyrics to songs your parents or guardians would definitely disapprove of?

- Do you share the entertainment likes of your friends? Have you even been with them and they were doing something you had no interest in but did it anyway because of your relationship? Now, there's nothing wrong with this if it's something positive and healthy. But if they were doing something you thought wasn't too cool, or even definitely something they shouldn't be doing, did you do it and put the risks involved in the back of your mind? Why and what was the outcome?
- Do you consider yourself a role model? Is someone you know looking up to you and following in your footsteps? Are you happy with what you see them imitate that comes from you? Has that person ever gotten in trouble for imitating something they saw you do?
- Do you care what impression you give to people you don't know? Why or why not?

Just say No

One day my aunt yelled for me to come downstairs to the family room. I thought maybe she needed me to kill a bug for her or tell me my grandmother was on the phone for me. However, when I got downstairs she said, "I just want you to know that you can get high off of life". I was like, uh...okay. "Do you understand what I'm saying?" I said "Yeah", and that was the end of that.

There are a number of commercials about perfect opportunities for parents to talk to their kids about drugs which are missed. I guess something made my aunt think about me and the possibility that I might get involved in drug use so she called me downstairs right then so she wouldn't let the opportunity pass. I still appreciate that moment, as simple and strange as it felt at the time.

Back in the 80s there was a TV slogan for drugs "Just Say No". But just saying no doesn't always apply. I never had the opportunity to say no because no one asked. There were plenty of kids smoking weed at the bus stop in the suburban area we lived in, but none of them ever even asked me to join them. I think it was because of the way they perceived me. I was the nerdy kid that didn't do anything to get in any real trouble because I was too scared. I didn't hang out with any other kids that smoked or drank, so I guess they figured what would be the use in even asking me. And I had a low opinion of the kids that smoked at the bus stop too. There was one in particular that did it frequently and I thought about the kind of student he was and how he acted most of the time and I didn't want to be compared to him in any way!

Most of us have someone in our families that has had issues with drugs or alcohol or both. I had a relative like this that was almost always in some kind of trouble at school because of drugs, either selling them or using them and he drank. He was one of the "black sheep" of the family. My family was always talking about something he did or would probably do. It would upset me in a number of ways because he was a great person to me. He was super- talented: track team, cross country team, football, basketball, and an excellent artist and writer. So hearing a bunch of mess about how bad he was, would only make me angry and want to defend him by telling them to look at all the good he was doing. Throughout his life, he battled with the grip that drugs and alcohol had on him and it was a vivid enough picture for me to understand that I didn't want to follow that path. He also told me never to let myself get involved with the things he was into. He didn't want to see me struggle the way he did. Even though he was so talented and had the opportunity to excel in anything he chose, his habits kept him from being the person he wanted to be.

Oh the many reasons kids decide to use drugs or drink, I can't list or even think of them all. However, it all boils down to decisions and choices. I don't know any statistics for the number of people that are *forced* to do drugs or take a drink, but I'm willing to guess that not many people fall into this category. It's a matter of it being presented and then them deciding what they wanted to do. Yes, there is peer pressure to consider; someone who's trying to convince you to join the club will be the best sales representative ever. They will give you all the information you need to make you feel it's one of the best thing you will ever experience. At the time that they are presenting this information, although it may be true for them, you have to understand that what it does for them, it may not do for you. It's like perfume. You can smell a certain perfume on someone and ask, "What are you wearing?" They tell you and you decide you want to smell like that too. So you get it, and start to wear it, and find that it smells totally different on you! That's because of your body chemistry, and the way it mixes with the perfume.

Drugs and alcohol are very much the same. They mix differently with each person. What it takes for one person to get high will not be the same for someone else.

Another thing that the drug and alcohol representative can't tell you is what the impact will be on your life right then, or even later. How will your use affect your family, friends, or your future?

Some people say, "Oh, I'll just try it this once to see what it's like and then I won't do it again." Addictions have no prejudices; they will take hold on the first try if they choose to and have you in a situation that takes years to heal from, or that may end up being the cause of your death.

If you feel like your life is so boring that you need to add some spice to it and feel like drugs or alcohol will improve it, you're in for a big surprise. With abusive substances, each time you use them you will need more the next time in order to attempt to get the high you originally felt. And the more you use, the more damage you're doing to your body and your life.

So, if you are given the opportunity to be introduced to drugs or alcohol, tell them you will think about it, and then do just that, THINK about it. While you are thinking do some research on the thing that they introduced to you, get all the facts about it and its effect on your body and your mind. Talk to someone about it, tell your parents you are considering doing drugs or drinking, or a teacher, or minister, see what they have to say about it. You'd be surprised if you actually talk to an adult and give them an opportunity to tell you about some of the things they've done in the past and how it affected them, or someone in their family. Check into your own family tree, see how the family deals with the relative that has an addiction and then put yourself in that picture, do you want to take their place?

So what do you think...

- Has anyone offered drugs or alcohol to you already? If not who do you think would and what do you plan on saying?
- Do you feel it's okay to try things just because the person who offers it seems to be cool and doesn't seem to be experiencing any negative affects?
- Do you consider yourself to be a risk taker? What kinds of things are you willing to risk losing? Are you willing to lose your family, friends, and money, your health?
- The kids at school that you know are into drugs and alcohol, what kind of students are they, do they do well or are they just getting by? If they have no problems at school, what do their home lives look like? The thing is, there are people who can appear to have it all together, even while they have a serious addiction, but if you can take a closer look you will see that it takes them a lot to hide their demons and keep up the appearance of success. Eventually the bottom falls out.
- If you can, try attending an ALANON meeting or an AA meeting, listen to the individual testimonies about how their lives have unfolded with an addiction that started out as just "experimenting."

Leather and Filled with Sand

What's leather and filled with sand? Probably a number of things, but I'm talking about a punching bag. And one thing that's not leather and filled with sand is you.

So why would you allow anyone to treat you like you are?

When I was working as a counselor I was shocked to find so many young ladies who had been abused by their boyfriends and believed that this was acceptable. They said things like, "I deserved it because I did this or that." "He doesn't do it all the time". "But I hit him back", and hosts of other "reasons" and excuses. But there is never a reason to allow any male to put his hands on you. Unless you attend a school that has co-ed wrestling or football, there should be no contact between a boyfriend and girlfriend that causes bruises, scratches, or any other bodily harm.

Unfortunately some of you that have seen females in your family be abused or maybe even have a friend that has experienced it. When you talk about the incidents you witnessed with these females they may create a picture that seems okay, and they might say things that make you feel they don't have a problem with the violence. They may tell you that violence and abuse are normal for relationships. If women you trust and love never told you that violence and abuse is wrong, you may be convinced that it isn't wrong. You may end up becoming a part of a vicious cycle just like they have. It's human nature to copy behaviors we feel are acceptable, this can be a good thing, or a bad thing.

I guess smoking could be a good example of a habit many people fall into from simply seeing someone else doing it. They may not be fully aware of the dangers when they first start smoking because they are just doing it because it seemed harmless enough. But once they become aware of its dangers, they may have already formed a habit that is extremely hard to break. Be careful of not listening to yourself; if you see or hear something that doesn't sound right, and makes you feel uncomfortable, it probably *isn't* right.

Abuse is a habit, for both the people doing it and the people who become victims of it. Sometimes it starts off very small and you don't even realize what's going on. He may just say things that are hurtful and you brush them off or he apologizes and you forgive him. Then later it grows to arguments and threats. Again, he apologizes or gives you something nice and you forgive him. Before long it's advanced to pushes and shoves and then full- fledged hands on conflicts. Sometimes he will apologize and go all out to make you feel it will never happen again and sometimes he may blame you and *you* end up apologizing!

Abuse is also a mental game. It's hard sometimes to know what you are experiencing. Sometimes you are not sure if someone is being abusive and you start to doubt and question yourself so much that you feel lost and confused. This confusion makes it easier for the abuser to brainwash you get you to believe everything is fine.

When I was 17 I had a boyfriend that was older than me and out of school already. He didn't come from the same city or state, so none of my immediate friends or family knew him. A guy that had graduated from my high school introduced us, and he was a really nice guy so I never thought a friend of his would be anything but a gentleman. My new boyfriend and I didn't see each other very often because he was usually gone someplace across the globe, he was in the military. He would send me the coolest gifts and call me and send me flowers and he always had something really nice to say about me. I was head over heels for this guy! I had a boyfriend who'd already graduated from high school, who was in the military and who seemed to think the world of me. Well, my uncle warned me that I shouldn't get all excited about someone I didn't really know. He told me that you can never really know someone unless you spend time with them. I didn't want to listen; I was head over heels and young in love. My uncle also told me one day, "Never stay with a man that puts his hands on you. Even if he *acts* like he's going to, eventually he will". Of course I wondered why he'd said this to me but it stuck in my mind. At that time the Oprah show was pretty new and I'd seen a number of women who'd talked about abuse and how they'd gotten stuck in the cycle and it almost cost them their lives. I also heard stories about women that didn't get out soon enough and were killed by someone that abused them. So I had all this knowledge in store just in case it happened to me. I felt there was no way I would stay with anyone that tried to hurt me, I said I wouldn't allow myself to be so in love that I'd be blind to abuse, I was smarter than that.

Well, I got my chance to test out this philosophy of mine, because my oh so wonderful boyfriend pushed me one day and threatened me, warning me not to try to get away from him. Oh my Lord! I thought I was trapped inside a nightmare! I couldn't believe it was happening. Flashbacks of everything my uncle warned me about flew up and all those Oprah shows were spinning around in my head. I was sick to my stomach that he could have behaved that way. Although it never got to the point that he hurt me, that incident was enough. I told some friends about it, and a family member to see what their reactions were. Even though in my heart I knew I could not be with him anymore, I wanted to see what other people saw in the incident. Yes, he told me he would never touch me like that again. And I wanted to believe him and I stayed with him a little while longer, can you believe it. But I couldn't trust that he wouldn't do it again because he had had the nerve to do it in the first place. I also took some time after the incident to watch how he treated other people, and I found out that he was very rude, mean and inconsiderate especially to other women.

So you see he wasn't the gentleman I thought he was, but I didn't know it until I got to spend time with him. Most of you will have plenty of time to spend with that special guy. So keep your eyes open and don't let those happy feelings and emotions get in the way of your common sense. If you see that he treats others poorly, he will eventually treat you the same way. If you know he has hit a female in the past, don't think he won't do it again. Don't make excuses for his behavior or allow him to make you feel you shouldn't question him about his behavior. Most abusive people will not admit that they are abusive, they will do all they can to make you change your mind about things you have seen with your own eyes.

If you are already in an abusive relationship, get help. Tell someone, a teacher, someone at church, a trusted family member or friend. The longer you wait the deeper and more dangerous the situation will become. If you know someone in an abusive relationship, do all you can to get them to understand the danger they are in. If they don't listen to you, you might want to have someone else get involved. Lots of friendships are torn apart when one friend tries to help another that doesn't want to be helped. You may lose a friend, but if it keeps her from making one of the biggest mistakes ever, you may have saved her life.

Before I forget…verbal abuse can be just as devastating as physical abuse. Having someone tell you how ugly, stupid and unwanted you are hurts just like being punched. Abusive guys love to use females to get a laugh out of their friends. They will say the cruelest and most hateful things in front of other people and when you question them about it or say it hurt you, they will say they were only kidding and had no intention of hurting you, and then they will turn around and do it all again later. There are some guys that treat you like a dog behind closed doors yet act like they love you to death when you're out in public. If your boyfriend, or any guy that claims they care for you does these things, the same rules apply as for physical abuse, LEAVE HIM ALONE!

It shouldn't hurt to be loved, or liked for that matter. Yes your heart may get broken when you fall for someone and things don't turn out right. But abuse should never be the reason for pain you may feel while being in a relationship. Understand that you are too valuable to allow anyone to treat you like a punching bag. Love yourself enough to save yourself from abuse.

Round One...

- Do you feel it's all right for a man to hit a woman, and if so, why?
- Have you had a boyfriend that hit you? What did you do afterwards?
- Did he apologize and say he'd never do it again? And if so, did you stay to find out? Did the cycle repeat itself over and over each time he has a more elaborate and wonderful make up for it?
- Has a female ever told you that it is all right for a man to hit you? If so, is she being abused by a male herself? What are her reasons for tolerating it and how do you feel when you know she's been hit? How do her scars and bruises affect you when you see them?

If you are still confused about what abuse it, call an abuse Hotline and talk to a counselor anonymously and listen to what they tell you. If you had to even question your own or someone else's situation, it is probably abuse. You have a right to be safe; so don't be afraid to reach out for help.

Let's Face It

There was a time in my past when strangers often said to me in passing, "Smile, it can't be that bad". It always surprised me, because I was not aware of the expression on my face until they said something to me about it. I may have been thinking about something and lost in thought, but at the time I never really considered what others might see when I'm just walking through the mall. It all boiled down to what my face and body language was putting out to the world. Nowadays I take care to put on the face I want people to see, one that will reflect who I am inside and not what I may be going through or thinking. I am a friendly person, I love to laugh and make others laugh. I also love to talk to people I don't know, sometimes just to see if maybe they need some cheering up. I'm almost always willing to strike up a conversation in a shopping line just to kill time. I've had some wonderful conversations and met some awesome people just by smiling and saying "Hello."

I know you all know the saying that "a first impression is a lasting impression". Well just imagine, you are going in for a job interview and just before going into the interview you got some really bad news. It had nothing to do with the job you were about to interview for, but it affected you nonetheless. You get into the manager's office and have this horrible scowl on your face. What do you think the manager is going to think? He or she has no idea about the news you heard prior to the interview, they just know that if you really wanted that job you would have presented yourself like it was the most important thing going on at that moment. Chances are you will not be selected after this type of first impression.

One day I went out to lunch with a friend. It took a while for the waitress to even get to our table. We had to flag someone down and let it be known that we needed to be served. When the waitress finally came to the table she looked like it was the last place she wanted to be. She gave us an insincere apology and said she was tired. I couldn't believe it! The entire time she waited on us it was like she was doing it because she was being forced. She had no concern that it was her job to make sure our dining experience was the best it could be. I hate doing this, but I couldn't even force myself to leave her a tip. My friend left the tip because she felt it was necessary because we'd been served but I disagreed. Why take a customer service position if you could care less about the customers?

It became a habit and practice of many young people some time ago to look "hard". I would typically see young men doing this the most. They put on this hard face, frowning and scowling like they really are mad about something and for some reason. This image is one that actually leads people to stereotype them saying they are hostile and probably dangerous to be around. These young men seemed to think that expressing peacefulness or happiness is being "soft". Young women that copy these mannerisms are stereotyped right along with the guys. It's difficult enough being a young adult as it is, why make things more difficult by giving people excuses to say bad things about you and associate you with trouble and bad behavior?

What you present to the world in body language is what you will more than likely receive in return. If you are frowning all the time, people will frown in return and keep away. If you smile and radiate happiness, people tend to respond with the same. It's a good idea not to allow what you are feeling inside to always reflect in your body language. Would you want a teacher who's having a rough day to stand in front of class looking like she had a rough day? How do you think it will affect the atmosphere in the classroom? If you know you need to change your attitude in order to change your body language, take time to regroup, think of things that will lighten your mood and go from there. If you pretend you are having good day long enough, it usually ends up turning around and becoming a good day.

I used to hate participating in group games when I worked at the youth alternative program. I always thought of the negative things that sometimes happened during the games and anticipated the worst so my attitude was terrible on game days. Then I started doing something I'd heard when I was in the military "fake it til you make it." I started actively participating in the group games acting like I was having fun... and very soon I actually DID have fun. I started volunteering to run the games and I had a ball and the kids began looking forward to me running the games. Even the kids that tried to ruin the fun had a hard time because the mood was so good.

So, start with the girl in the mirror. What do you want her to present to the world, and what do you want her to get in return? Whatever it is put it on her face.

Whatchu looking at...

- Has anyone ever said, "Smile it's not that bad" to you more than a few times? If so, did you understand what they meant by the comment, or were you already aware of the expression you held?

- What kind of person would you most likely respond to or attempt to strike up a conversation with? What kind of body language would they have to have for you to do this? Is it the kind of body language you have most of the time?

- Has your body language ever gotten you in trouble? I can recall times when I was told, "don't look at me like that" when I was in trouble, has this ever been said to you?
- Did your body language at the time you were being confronted by a teacher, parent or other authority figure, make the problem worse?

- Do you think that looking "hard" image is cool? Do you do it? When you do, how do people outside of your peer group tend to treat you, look at your and respond to you?

- If this isn't an area of concern for you, why do you think it isn't?

Lip Service

Do you like to talk? I do. I know sometimes I talk a LOT, maybe too much. But talking a lot is not the same as communicating effectively. There are tons of people that struggle with communication; be it expressing their feelings, speaking in front of groups, or writing a paper for a class. There are lots of different types of communication: phone, written word, one on one discussion, body language... But let's focus on one: telling people how you feel.

I've had people tell me that they don't have to worry about wondering what's on my mind because I don't seem to have a problem saying it. When something isn't right, I will usually let someone know one way or another. If someone asks for my opinion, they will get it, but not before I ask if they are sure they really want the truth. I wear most of my feelings on my face. If I am upset, you will see it, if I'm hurting you will see it, or even hear it in my voice. Sometimes I wish people could really read my body language so I wouldn't have to SAY anything. There are two parts to communication: sending and receiving. Some people are good about sending out information, but don't receive it well; they can talk all day about how they feel, but can't listen to anyone else's feelings. Then there are people who are excellent listeners but can't say what they have on their minds. I try to do well with both. Of course, I'm not always successful with this, but I try hard to be aware of what kind of listener and speaker I am.

There are times when it's hard to tell people things. You may be afraid what you have to say will upset them somehow. Sometimes you just can't gather the words that will express what you feel. Sometimes you just feel that what you have to say may not be important, or that it will not be taken seriously or have the result you desire, so you hold everything inside.

There are no perfect ways to communicate. We all have our own different ways. Of course there are some good and bad ways though. You can't yell at people and expect positive results; unless you are trying to warn someone about something that will save them from harm (a car is coming and they are in the street). There are no techniques that will be foolproof either; sometimes the style you choose to express yourself may work great, but other times it just may not. There are risks involved when you are going to communicate and you have to be willing to accept some failures and not celebrate too much with the victories.

One time I got really upset with a friend of mine. I was hurt, mad, disappointed, and had a million things to say. So I wrote everything down in a letter and gave it to her. The letter allowed me to organize my thoughts and make sure I said everything I wanted to. When I told a family member what I had done, they felt I shouldn't have chosen this way to express myself. They said that writing a letter is ONE WAY communication that doesn't allow the receiver to respond. I felt trapped then, I felt like I was being more hurtful than effective in trying to resolve a problem. The thing is, just because he didn't agree with my method didn't make it wrong. It was the best way I could express myself and my friend and I were able to talk about the things I'd written. I didn't write the letter to just vent and not expect a response, I wanted to hear her side however she chose to give it to me. I still write letters to people that I have a hard time talking to and in the letters I usually let them know that it was easier for me to write it than to talk on the phone or in person. I do this especially when the person lives far away from me or if I've had confrontations with them in the past and talking couldn't resolve any issues. Yes, some of my letters have made situations worse, that was the risk I had to take, but at least I tried.

I've had some successes with just asking people to sit down and talk to me. Sometimes the end result was far better than I expected. And there have been times when talking turned into arguing and the situation ended up way worse than it started.

The point is you want to at least make an effort to communicate with people when you have something you want to express. I don't know many people that can read minds or body language and know exactly what's going on. This is especially true when you know that the issue is tearing you up inside. You may have to talk to yourself, have a conversation in the mirror practicing what you will say and how you want your face to look. You may have to hold something in your hand while you talk, squeezing it while you get things off your chest. Ask someone to help you, have them listen while you talk to them pretending they are the person you really want to talk to.

There are so many ways to communicate effectively. You must be willing to stumble through some ways that don't work until you get it right. You must know that you will have to use different techniques for different situations and people. And you must be strong enough to even TRY most of all. Letting things build up inside is never good for you, mentally or physically. So let it out, keeping in mind how **you** would like to be addressed: respectfully, tactfully, honestly, calmly, sensitively, lovingly, fairly, kindly, and gently.

Sometimes it is best to remain quiet. When you know you are not able to control your feelings, or if you are extremely angry. Sometimes when we speak too soon we end up saying things we regret. You have to attempt to judge when the best time is to speak.

And finally sometimes it is best to not express yourself at all. Sometimes issues are resolved with silence. In time you will learn which method works for which situations. Hopefully you will also be able to build confidence in your ability to speak your mind respectfully and effectively.

Come and talk to me...
- How effectively do you feel you communicate, in spoken word and written word?
- If you communicate well, has this always been the case? If not, what do you feel you need to improve your communication skills?
- If you have had problems communicating, do you know why? What have you been told when you've tried to communicate: I don't understand, get to the point, speak up, slow down, hurry up, that's not the right word, you're repeating yourself...anything along these lines?
- Have you asked anyone for help when you've struggled, like a teacher, parent, or someone you feel has good communication skills? You'd be surprised how willing people are to be test subjects when you need help.
- Have you tried different techniques when you worry you won't be able to actually talk to someone? I cry pretty easily, especially when I'm upset. I know this, so if I have to confront someone I practice what I will say, or I write a small note with the topics I need to address so I don't talk longer than I should. I take the note card or sticky note with me when I talk to the person.

***If you are a letter writer like me, make sure you do spell check and read what you have written a few times before handing it off. Spelling or really bad grammatical mistakes will take away from the effectiveness of the letter! And remember...texting and letters don't always provide enough information for the person to really know what you're trying to say. Talking in person is the best way to do this, even though it's the hardest.

***Don't do anything while you are angry! It may cause you to do or say things you wish you never had. Cool off and then start the task.

Lost and Found

There was this really big wooden box in the basement of my elementary school that was the Lost and Found. Whenever I lost anything I would go there to see if it was put in the box. I never found my own things, but there were always some pretty good things there, one sock out of a pair, one glove, one shoe, a hat...stuff like that. You can find some pretty good things in a lost and found box, but one thing I never found was a friend.

Hopefully, throughout your life you will find a friend or two. Some people have lots of friends; some people only have a few. I realized when I was in my twenties that the reason I didn't have a whole lot of friends was because I felt like it was too hard to share myself with a number of people. I liked to be very open with my friends and to be able to talk to them about anything. I felt like if I had a bunch of friends there would be a bunch of people that knew a lot about me and I'd be sort of spread out in pieces. Some people can handle having lots of friends, they know how to manage their time so none of them feel left out. Sometimes people say others are their friends, but they really have no true commitment to them. I've seen people say the worst things about people they call a friend, yet when that person is around they are sweet as sugar to them. Being "Two-Faced" is what that's called.

Many people have a circle of friends. The circle can be large or very small. You will have to know what kind of person you are to know what kind of people will be good friends for you. Like I said, my circle is pretty small. I know that I must have friends that can keep my business to themselves, and they know that I will do the same for them. They have to be good listeners because I talk a lot and tend to drift from one topic to another, if they can't handle this, there will be a problem. It's nice if we share similar interests but it's also good to be able to learn from each other because of the things that differ between us. A good friend does not need to be a clone of you; having differences in tastes can help each of you broaden your horizons. But if the differences you have are a source of tension, you may want to consider how much you value the friendship or if it is a healthy friendship.

Let's say you are a pretty conservative dresser, you keep things comfortable and simple. You may have a friend that likes clothes that fit very tight and show a lot of skin. You have a problem with it. You have told her about it and expressed yourself in a loving way, but she's not hearing it. Now you have to decide, are you willing to compromise, be her friend regardless of how she dresses? She may be an awesome person to you and you may be able to get over her tastes in clothes. But then again, the clothes may be something you can't handle and you end up losing the friendship.

There's a saying that a friend is someone that knows all your secrets and failures and still loves you anyway. Being a friend is an ongoing process. As you mature you learn more about yourself and the people around you and you will more than likely make changes in the people you choose to share company with. That can be hard at times because we don't all mature the same way. You may have been the kind of person that loved loud music and trips to the mall every weekend. But as time went on you lost interest in those things and your friends did not. And then you find yourself hanging out with a different group of friends or even spending more time by yourself. It's just life going through its cycles. People will come and go and you will hurt when some of them leave and others you may not be able to wait for them to leave! You'll lose some friends and find some new ones.

But you also have to know how to *be* a friend. If you decide that you will be a friend to someone, don't expect more from him or her than you are willing to give. Don't promise them things that you know you don't plan on delivering. You have to be able to listen to their needs and accept some constructive criticism from them. If they truly love you their goal is to have you be as successful in life as they want themselves to be, so they will do their best to try to catch you if you start to fall and vice versa. Yes you will disagree at times, you may get into a huge fight even, but sometimes those disagreements can be tools for growth. You have to choose what you will tolerate and what you think is more than you can handle.

That Two- Faced person I mentioned earlier is a hard one to handle. Sometimes you aren't aware that someone is being a hater behind your back, even if someone tells you, you may not want to accept it. Sometimes a person that has bad intentions for you will do all they can to get close to you. They will find out everything about you and know your strengths and weaknesses so they can use them against you. If you suspect that a friend is doing this to you, be careful. If you catch them in the act, don't let the pain blind you, value yourself enough to walk away. One time while I was in college I went home for the weekend. When I came back I walked to my room I heard some girls talking, they were tearing someone to pieces saying all kinds of nasty things. I realized that they were talking about me. I went into my room and cried but I didn't say anything because I wanted to see how they treated me once they found out I was back. They were all smiles and compliments when they finally saw me, and I knew that I needed to keep my distance to a certain extent and be careful about what I said and did around them from then on. There's another saying, keep your friends close, and your enemies closer, meaning, sometimes you need to be aware of the people that would do you wrong, it keeps you ahead of their games.

Research shows that having a good friend can extend your life. When you have someone that shares your life in a positive and nurturing way your health is improved. So choose good friends, and be a good friend. But don't short yourself by holding on to friends that don't have your best interests at heart. If you can't shake the feeling that a friend may not *really* be a friend, they probably aren't.

A Friend Indeed

- How do you choose your friends?
- What are the similarities and differences that make your friendships special?
- Do you feel confident that they will have your back if you need them?
- Do they support your decisions and help you be the best you can be, even if it means telling you something you may not like?
- What kinds of things would cause you to not want to be that person's friend in the future?
- If a friend hurts you, can you tell them? If not, why?
- How would you rate yourself as a friend? What do you feel you could work on?
- Do you have friends that only come around when they need something from you, but never available when you need them? This is called a "fair weather" friend. Are you the fair weather type...expecting things from others when you need them, but don't make time for them?

Making Up

I believe I was in the 11th grade when I got really interested in wearing makeup. I'm not sure if the smooth, soft eyeliner was invented yet because all the girls at school had to use a lighter or a match to soften it up before they could use it. I got a small stick of eyeliner from a friend when I saw her putting some on in the bathroom one day. I put some on, but I made sure I wiped it off before I got home. But then I asked my aunt if it was all right for me to use it, surprisingly she said yes. I kept things pretty simple (eye liner and lip gloss) because I didn't have money to get a bunch of stuff and didn't know how to use much of anything else anyway.

The feeling of seeing yourself in a whole new way can be fun and exciting! I love to try out a new colors of lip gloss and eye colors! Don't be ashamed of wanting to upgrade your looks a little. Remember however, that cosmetics don't make you pretty, you are pretty all on your own; make up simply compliments what God has already done. Some ladies wear a full suit of makeup and underneath their skin is flawless and beautiful. Some ladies wear make up to cover up blemishes and scars. You have to be careful to clean your face before and after you wear makeup. Putting it on dirty skin locks the dirt deeper in your pores and contaminates your applicator brushes, so you are just putting dirt on your face over and over which will cause you to have breakouts/acne. If you already have acne, it will only make things worse! Clean the brushes as well as your skin.

Okay, let's look at the words themselves: Make Up. To makeup means to re-do, to do again, or to pretend, or invent. Why would anyone want to "make up" a face? I believe that makeup should accentuate or spruce up what you already have. For the most part the trend in makeup is the barest of bare, just light accents and not heavy coats of color. Who knows how long this will be the trend in fashion, but I like this look for myself. I also like the dramatic looks that other women are able to wear. I guess how you use make up tends to match your personality. It's nice to experiment and look for colors that bring out something in your face, like your eye color, or your lips and cheekbones. I've seen young ladies lay on the eye shadow pretty heavy to bring out their eye color, but there are much more attractive ways to do this. If you aren't sure what will work best on your complexion or with the colors of your eyes and hair etc., choose a cosmetic counter at the mall and ask the representative to help you out. It's a free make over and if you don't like it you haven't spent any money. The cosmetic representative will give you a look she creates unless you tell her what you want. You may like what he or she does, you may not. And if you do like it, it doesn't mean you have to purchase the products the representative applied. You can learn how to apply and remove the products there was well. And you can typically find inexpensive cosmetics that work just as good as some of the expensive ones.

Now, let me go back to something I said earlier about my first experience with makeup: I used someone else's stuff. Not good! You can do some serious damage to your skin when you share makeup, and you can pass along lots of bacteria and germs that will get you sick or cause infections. So, use your own stuff and don't be afraid to just say "No" when one of your friends wants to borrow your stuff. And another thing, I removed the eyeliner before my family saw it...wrong wrong wrong. I was being deceitful basically because I'd done something I wasn't sure my family would approve of. I didn't want to keep doing that so I made sure I got permission right away. There are plenty of young ladies that ask for things and don't get their way, so they go to school one way, then change, then change again when it's time to go home. This is wrong and deceitful. Whoever told them "no" had a reason. So be respectful of whoever has authority over the way you appear for school. There are plenty of very young girls wearing makeup and this is a fact some young ladies will try to use when they ask if they can do it too, "Jo Jo's mother lets HER wear it!" Don't go there either. There's a time and place for everything. Be careful of trying to rush into things that seem like no big deal to you but your family makes a big deal of when it's brought up. Just know that in time you will be able to make your own decisions and be respectful of what you are asked while you are still living at home. Take your time and bloom naturally, like the flower you are.

Make me over...

- If you want to wear makeup, why?
- What do your parents or guardians have to say about it?
- How do you think it will affect your relationships with your friends?
- Are you doing it to get the attention of someone?
- Do you think you are attractive now, or that the makeup will make you attractive?
- When you think about what you want to look like, WHO do you think about? Do you have some favorite celebrity whose look you admire? Or maybe someone you know?
- What is it about their style that you like?
- If you already wear makeup, how does it make you feel? Do you feel better about yourself when you wear it? Do you feel you have to have on make up when you leave the house or are you just as comfortable and confident with your appearance without it?

Mama, Oh No Not Mia

I had a friend in high school that I thought was one of the coolest people ever. She appreciated my silliness and would ask me to do things that made her laugh. She accepted me for who I was and never made fun of me or tried to humiliate me. She trusted me with information and introduced me to her mom with pride. I thought we were very much alike and so I was totally shocked when she told me one day that she was pregnant. I didn't know what to say or do. I wasn't sure how to be supportive and continue to be her friend. I was confused by the situation. I couldn't possibly imagine her having sex and oh my God, she was going to have a baby! She was incredibly smart and very mature. She had everything all planned out and I admired that. She opted to graduate early, since she had enough credits and she knew that staying at school would be too stressful. We were seniors, so we were legally adults, but in my mind I still felt like a child and knew there was no way I would have been able to manage being an 18-year old mother. I never got to talk to her again after she left school and that was sad. I was confident that she would do well for herself though. I couldn't see it coming out any other way. I should have really thought about all the things I admired about her and chose those reasons to remain her friend rather than feel that we were too different to be friends.

Why my friend chose to have a child I will never know. Maybe it was something she hadn't planned but once it happened she made choices for her life that she was comfortable with. However, there are so many other young women that don't approach having children the same way. One of the scariest things I've heard is a young woman saying that she wanted to have a child so that she would have someone to love and someone that loved her back. Whoa! I was thinking, adopt a cat or a dog, they will suffice rather than creating another person. The amount of care and responsibility that comes with having a child is often a challenge women and men in their 30s can barely handle. So what makes a teenager chose to voluntarily have a child and think it's not going to be hard?

Now look, as with the case of my friend, maybe it wasn't a planned event, but she had a choice to make. She knew what she could handle and did what she thought was best for her. She had a very good bond with her mother who was willing to help and guide her. I'm sure my friend talked to her mother and they made some plans together. Many young women assume that their mothers will either help take care of a child they have, or will be the sole caregiver for the child. Everything is fine and dandy while the girl is pregnant. She's putting it all together in her mind and thinking about how wonderful it's going to be to have this little baby that needs and loves her. But then, once the baby is born and she sees all the work that's required, she swiftly turns everything over to her mother and decides she'd rather hang out with her friends and just be a regular teenager again. This is so unfair. That young woman's mother has already been through the ordeal of birthing and raising a child, and she may not want to do it again. I was watching the news one day and they were covering a story about a woman who was in her late 60s struggling to raise 4 small children that belonged to her daughter. This woman was getting some assistance from the state but it was often not even enough to provide the children with balanced meals. Every time the woman's daughter had a child, she would end up raising that child. The woman didn't want to tell her daughter to stop bringing the children to her because she was afraid of what might happen to them if she didn't care for them; if they ended up in another home they may not even get the little bit of care that she was able to provide.

My friend had no plans on heavily depending on her mother to care for the child because she knew the baby was not her mother's responsibility, it was her own. There are a number of young women that get pregnant a little ways off from their senior year. These young women may not always have the option to just graduate early. They must find ways to balance being a new mother and finishing school. Many of these young women do it wonderfully. There are programs that help teen mothers finish school, work and care for their children. These young women are determined to reach goals they have set for themselves, regardless of the obstacles. It's always inspiring to hear the stories of these young mothers, it shows me that I don't really have an excuse for not trying to succeed when these young women can do it with the cards stacked against them.

If you are curious about what it would be like to care for a child, try babysitting for someone. Some schools have a program that provides a baby doll that is programmed to be like a real baby: it cries and has to be changed and fed. Students are given the "child" for a day or parts of a school day and are graded on how well they care for the child. It's not as easy as it may seem! So imagine what it's like to care for a real baby, that's home with you and costs money to care for!

So if you even get the idea in your head that having a child will be the answer to your need for acceptance, love, attention, company, a sense of accomplishment...whatever, just start looking for a very high maintenance cat or dog instead. If you have a friend who's thinking she wants a baby to fulfill those needs, suggest the cat or dog for her. And if you have a friend who's already pregnant, don't run away from her, be supportive, and try to keep being her friend. You never know how much you can learn about a person or yourself when there's a really difficult challenge to face.

I originally wanted to have a child in my early twenties. Fortunately, this didn't happen because I may have missed out on some wonderful opportunities if I'd had a child to care for. Besides that, I was honestly not mature enough to do the things I needed for a baby, I wasn't even taking care of myself to the best of my abilities. Even today, I know that there are still some things I want to accomplish before I can give my whole self to a child. Until that time comes I will be buying cat, fish, dog, or bird food instead of baby food!

Wishful thinking...

- Have you considered getting pregnant in the near future? Why?
- How would having a child now affect your life? Would it help you achieve any of the goals you have set for yourself?
- Do you have a friend that is pregnant or already has a child? If so, what kind of life does she have? Who provides care for the child when she is at school, if she is still in school? Is she happy to be a mother? Does she spend quality time with the child and do her best to give it the things it needs to be healthy mentally and physically?
- If you have a desire for a baby, is it to feel loved and needed? If so do you know that you could fulfill these needs in other ways, like church, Boys and Girls Club, volunteering at a hospital or nursing home or daycare center?

- Do you have the idea that having a child could help financially? There are some women who have children so that they can receive financial assistance from the state, but who don't care for the children with the money they receive. A child is not a paycheck! It is a living being in need of love and nourishment, development and dedication. So many children grow up feeling unwanted and without the tools they need to be successful. They sometimes have lives filled with violence and crime because they feel they have to take or steal things they want or need all because they weren't taught the best ways to survive or achieve goals.
- If you are not willing to give your child the life it deserves, it is best not to intentionally bring them into this world. Remember, no child ever ASKS to be created.
- What kind of mother do you want to be? What kind of mother do you feel is the ideal mother? Can you be that kind of mother for a child right now, even on the smallest of scales? If not, why even attempt?

Move Your Body

Hide and go seek, Mother May I, Four Square, Tag, Dodge Ball, Explorers, Duck Duck Goose...I could go on and on. Do any of these games sound familiar to you? Do you play them now or have you ever? These games were almost a daily occurrence for me as a child. If I wasn't playing them when I was at school, I was playing them when I got home. I was outside most of the time when it was warm enough and when it was cold I had plenty of clothes to wear that would allow me to get out and have fun. I would snow sled on cardboard boxes when we moved out of the city to the suburbs. I ran and jumped and rode bikes and skateboards and took long walks just to see what there was to see. I climbed trees, shoveled snow, cut grass, did yard work...okay where am I going with all this you ask? I kept busy when I was young. Actively moving my body and getting exercise without even knowing it. I was a lean, mean, fighting machine and had no idea how lucky I was. Yes, there were video games then. I was a part of the first generation of video gamers. There was Atari, which is the mother to all the video games now. There were hand held games that were entertaining and educational. I had a Little Professor, it helped you with math skills and I loved that thing. I also had a hand held football game that I loved just as much. But neither of those games could hold a candle to riding my bike over 30 miles per hour down the steep street in our neighborhood. Even when I fell at the bottom of that hill in front of a group of kids, I just got up, got back on and lived to do it again.

I am saying all this because it seems nowadays kids don't even know how to go outside and play. When they talk about playing it's playing a video game. Sitting in front of a TV working your fingers and wrists is not exercise. I know, I know, who wants to exercise at your age?! But just take a look around you, how many kids do you see that are overweight? How many kids get made fun of because they are overweight? You may be one of them. So what is it that needs to change: your level of physical activity or maybe your eating habits or both? Video games are great for hand-eye coordination. However, hand-eye coordination is not going to keep you from getting bit when a stray dog comes chasing you; you will be too out of breath once you start running to save yourself.

In all my schools, we had gyms that were fully equipped: balls, mats, ladders, you name it and we had it. Gym or physical education was mandatory; you had to have so many hours of it to graduate. It's not like that now. For any number of reasons many schools have changed their requirements and in some cases had budget cuts and Gym class or PE got hit. The effects of this will ripple into generations to come.

Did you know that Americans are the most overweight people in the world? Due to our eating habits and lack of exercise we are more often the victims of diseases like diabetes, heart attack and stroke than people in other countries. Add to this the fact that some of these diseases are hereditary, and you've got double trouble.

My family has a history of diabetes. I have no desire to be diabetic. So guess what? I changed my diet and I stayed in the military even after my contract was up so that I HAD to stay in shape. I know that on my own I am kind of lazy and I will not put serious effort into exercising until I get past a comfortable weight. But that's silly, why not exercise regularly to keep from getting to a point where I have to work twice as hard to just get the weight off and get back in my clothes?

Okay, this is not as hard as you think, and you don't have to give up the video games. If you are not already involved in sports at school or in your community and have no idea how to get exercise without it being a drag, here are some simple steps to take just to get started:

1. Walk: if you are within walking distance of school, then walk. Even if there is a bus service, walk. Walking is one of the best known exercises and it allows you to really see what's around you. I have driven to places time and again, but once I walked those distances, I saw stuff I'd never noticed. Walk the dog or someone else's dog. Get the family involved, walk together someplace. We used to walk for miles around the city when I was young and I loved it. It never felt like exercise, it was just really cool seeing things from a different perspective.

2. Do your chores. Oh, the horror, right? But look, vacuuming uses a good amount of energy, especially if your vacuum is one of those old ones and kind of heavy. Working in the yard is awesome exercise, cutting grass and raking leaves and sweeping will get your heart pumping and burn calories. If you live in the north, get out the shovel and get that snow out of the way. Now, here's a tip and an incentive too if you like money: do chores for your neighbors. Crazy huh? But it works. Take advantage of the lazy kids in your neighborhood and do their work for cash. There was a guy at my high school that used to cut our grass and my aunt paid him well. When I cut the grass I didn't get jack, so think how you can clean up in the spring and summers. This same guy shoveled snow too.

3. Play hard. There are so many different things to do outside, get out and do them. Sometimes the smaller kids will be out playing while the older kids are inside playing video games. Play

with the little kids, they will wear you out and you'll be having fun at the same time. You can't beat that.

Come up with some things on your own that you can convert to exercise. Do some research; find out what you are supposed to weigh for your age and compare it to what you do weigh. Then plan an attack if you aren't where you should be or want to be. Attack the fat. Don't be a couch potato! Whatever you can do now will save you from dealing with all the problems that could come up later.

One, two, three, what's it gonna be?

- What kind of health history does your family have?
- Can you run a flight of steps without having to stop to catch your breath?
- How much time to you spend in front of the TV?
- When was the last time you worked up a good sweat?
- Are you involved in any type of athletic activity? If not, why?
- What kind of shape do you want to be in now and later?
- Have you ever even thought about your health, your weight and how important it is?

- I know sometimes a child has no control over certain things. If your family has habits that cause the whole family to be overweight you may not be able to choose what you eat. However, you can choose to be more active and you can ask your family to try to change so that everyone benefits.

Passion's Fruit

I think we are all born with passions, drives, and desires to fulfill inside us. Attempting to produce fruit from these passions is what defines many people. We remember people who do things we find exciting or extraordinary like climbing mountains, singing a great song, writing a book that we love or for creating something really cool, or even making changes that affect the entire world.

We also remember and admire people that do things every day that are huge in the way they impact our lives; people that fight fires, deliver babies, read stories to groups of children or help people in the community. The passions in us can be ignited and put into action, or they can sit inside us and rot. We can share them with the world, or take them to our graves. We can live lives that we can look back on and be proud of, or lives filled with regrets.

There are some things I've always wanted to do and every time I fail to attempt them, this sense of nagging bitterness grows inside me. This feeling is intensified if I see someone else attempt that same thing and be successful in it! The other day I was reading a magazine and saw a short article on a woman who began a program for young women to teach them some life essentials, ways to deal with their lives positively in the midst of all the chaos around them. She compared the idea of growing into womanhood with the life cycle of a butterfly and it became the central theme for her program. As I read this my mouth just dropped open! I said aloud: "That's the same thing I thought and wrote in my introduction to this book!" I have been trying to complete this project for much longer than I felt it should have taken. However, that might not be the case; my feelings of procrastination may have been unwarranted because there are some things I would have missed out on writing if I'd decided to publish this sooner. I have had some more experiences to go through in order for me to be able to share them here. Maybe seeing that article was God's way of letting me know that I need to get moving, that it was time to put the pedal to the medal and hit the home stretch for the finish line. So although I feel like some of the things I've envisioned were also a part of another person's passion, it's all good because in the end it is the intention behind it all that means the most. All the intention in the world means nothing, if you don't act on it.

There is a story in the Bible of a group of men who were given "talents." These talents were *money* in the story, but they can also be seen as gifts of talent we are blessed with. One of the men in the story did not use his talents the way he should have, and so they were taken away from him and given to someone else. I can only imagine how ashamed and angry this man was because that's sort of what it felt like to see my idea used by someone else. If I don't use the gifts God has given me, I can't get mad when I see someone else using them.

Plant the seeds you have, take action on the dreams you have, use the gifts you have. Whatever is in your soul, the core of your existence that burns inside you to do, do it! There may be people who try to make you feel stupid for attempting to fulfill your dream, but they may be the same people that need the invention you created, that medicine you discovered, that paint color you manufactured, that greeting card you designed. Living out your passions can make you rich financially and spiritually. So may your baskets run over with evidence of successful fruit production!

Juicy Stuff
- What are some of your passions?
- Have you already fulfilled some of them; if so, how did you feel once you saw the end result?
- Do you share your thoughts about these passions with people? What is their response? Does their response keep you from attempting these things?
- What keeps you from attempting to go after your passions?
- What drives you to attempt them?
- Have you written out a plan of action? Have you asked for help from anyone? Have you researched the idea and seen the positive possibilities?

*Note: there are lots of resources out there that will give you some guidance on how to put your plans to action. Believe me, whatever you might want to do, someone has probably done it or even written a book about it! That doesn't mean that what you want to do will be just another version of the same thing. How you put your impression on things is what matters. And your idea may end up being the first of its kind! There are lots of people that make shirts, but not all shirts are the same and there will be plenty of new types of shirts made in the future!

Seeds Of Doubt

When I was young, I used to lie a lot. Not about anything big, just stupid, small stuff. But the thing was, I would get in so much trouble once the lie was found out, it was ridiculous to keep it up. So one day, I vowed never to lie again. Of course this didn't mean anything to my family at first because no matter what I said, they thought I was lying. It took some time for them to gain trust in me and once they did, my life was simpler and I was given more responsibility. My family didn't have to worry about me not being where I said I was going to be or what my responses would be if they confronted me with something. Even today I still find no use for lying. I am always afraid that if I tell that little lie, it will blow up on me, and I will somehow end up having to own up to the truth of the matter and in an embarrassing way. I also can't stand to deal with people who are not honest. Once I hear someone lie, or see them commit a deceitful act, I lose respect for them.

There are too many consequences when you decide to be dishonest. You spend a lot of time worrying that you will get found out. You have to come up with more lies to cover the ones you told. If you are a heavy liar you get lost in the lies you told and can't get your stories straight after a while. Once you plant those seeds of doubt, you never really know what they will grow to become. How big will the thing get? The end result is usually the same; losing a friend, losing a job, losing your civil liberties (jail). You just never know!

Another consequence is the loss of trust. I value being reliable and trustworthy; it feels good to know people have confidence in me and respect my integrity. You can't get very far without trust and I'm not just talking about with friends and family. The bank has to trust you to give you a loan. The company you work for has to trust that you are able to do the job you said you can do. Your pets trust you to feed them. Once people discover that you cannot be trusted, it shuts you off from so many things. One lie or dishonest act can ruin a good part of your life. Some people spend years trying to earn back the trust that they have lost from a single incident.

Lying is really based on your decisions and choices. It's up to you to decide what kind of person you want to be. We all make mistakes, we live and we learn. If you made the mistake of being dishonest and had some negative consequences, that's the time to decide how you want your future to unfold: keep being dishonest and suffering or own up and give it up. Some people just like the thrill of being dishonest and getting away with it. What they don't realize is their dishonestly will eventually catch up with them. I can't see the appeal of constantly having a cloud following me around, never knowing when the bottom will drop out and how bad it will rain when it does!

Honesty is one of the greatest characters to have. It makes your life simpler, in the fact that you have hidden nothing. It is also hard sometimes to be honest when you know it may hurt someone's feelings. That is where tact (choosing your words carefully and with consideration) comes into play. For example someone asks you if they look fat or how they look period. If your response will hurt them, you have to find a way to do it with tenderness, as you would want someone to do for you. Sometimes honesty causes people to lose friends. Sometimes your friends will expect you to lie for them or do things that are dishonest to stay friends. Exercise good judgment in these situations! You could lie for a friend and end up paying the price that they should have paid. If they expect you to lie for them, it means they would readily lie on YOU to keep themselves out of trouble. Someone with a deceitful character uses it in many different ways, so be careful!

Mold your character into a good one. Make choices that keep your life simple and peaceful. Once you plant seeds of doubt you have to deal with what they grow to become.

Character Check:

- What kind of people do you admire; honest ones or ones that can tell a great lie and get away with it?
- Do you consider yourself an honest person?
- How do you feel when you are lied to?
- How do you feel when you see or hear someone do something dishonest? Does it upset you, make you laugh, or do you not really care?
- Who is the most honest person you know? Do you like that person, if so why? If not, why?
- Who is the most dishonest person you know or have known? What kind of relationship do you have with them?
- Have any of your friends ever asked you to do something dishonest for the sake of your friendship? Did you do it? What happened?
- Have you ever been honest about something and it made you feel really good?
- Have you ever been honest about something and it hurt someone and you felt bad? What did you do to try to make things better or what could you do the next time?

So Fresh...So Clean

There was a young lady in my homeroom in high school that had a problem and didn't seem to know it. She had an "odor" about her. It was so bad that other girls talked about it and were trying to figure out what to do. Me, being the writer that I am, suggested that they write her an anonymous note and leave it in her locker. Well, she didn't take it well. I believe her feelings were hurt and she suspected who'd left the note. If we had gone to her and spoken to her face- to –face, would that have been any better? Who knows, it was such a touchy situation.

In health classes during junior and senior high we learned that our hormones were changing, and we were becoming women. We learned about menstrual cycles and how babies were created and a host of other necessary information. Even with all the classes and even some open talks about the coming of puberty, the subject of how to take care of our bodies was not talked about in depth or sometimes at all. I had to learn a lot of things on my own and unfortunately, sometimes through being embarrassed at times.

When the chemical makeup of our bodies changes we need to adopt new knowledge and habits of cleanliness. It was fine as an elementary school kid to not use deodorant because we didn't put out any real funk that needed to be fought. When you notice that things are beginning to look and feel different on your body, it's time to make some changes in your daily routine. Deodorant is just a small part of the battle. The most effective way to combat the "change" is good old soap and water. You have to bathe every day; there are no ifs, ands or buts about it. There are plenty of fruity smelling, girly, shower gels, body glitters, and lotions out there, but you should get CLEAN first, then maybe add all the extras. It's like dessert, you have to eat the main meal first then you can have the sweet stuff. Getting your body clean takes some time and effort. You can't just rush through it and avoid major areas that will increase the possibility of an embarrassing event. What are these areas:

1. Vagina- it must be cleaned thoroughly, the outside and inner folds. Sweat collects in these areas and when it is not properly cleaned bacteria will build up and cause some really outstanding odors as well as set you up for an infection. Be careful if you put powder in your underwear, it can block pores and also disrupt the natural functioning of the vagina. The vagina is somewhat like a self-cleaning oven. It flushes itself out continually: that is called discharge. Discharge is NORMAL. When the discharge does not smell bad and is not darker than a light yellow, things are more than likely running smooth. But if the discharge has a foul odor and isn't the color it should be, you need to pay close attention to what's going on down there. Wearing tight clothing or underwear will wreak havoc on your vagina. It needs to breathe. You wouldn't wear a tight cloth around your mouth all day would you? Imagine what your breath would be like if you did that! It's the same case with your vagina. Fruity washes aren't good down there either. Unless the wash is an all-natural wash with no dyes or perfumes it may do more harm than good by causing chemical imbalances that will lead to problems later. Just use a regular deodorant soap or gentle cleansing wash and be sure to rinse well and dry completely.

- A note about douches. Douching is not recommended as a regular cleansing routine. Douching washes away the good bacteria in your vagina. If you feel you must do it, particularly after your menstrual cycle, chose one with simply vinegar and water.

2. **Underarms-** I'm sure you already know how rough they can get. It's an area most commonly associated with funk. So, wash, dry completely and put on that deodorant! Choose a deodorant that works well with your body. Sometimes it's a lot of trial and error finding a deodorant that works for you. Sometimes you have to change it with the season: one deodorant for winter, one for summer, for example. There are also all natural deodorants. I choose these because they lack certain chemicals that are not good for you. Powder here is cool, just make sure you don't overdo it when wearing a tank top or other sleeveless shirt. We all develop at different times. I had hair in private places when I was really young and it was embarrassing sometimes because other girls would comment on it. I didn't know about shaving under my arms until I found out one of my cousins was shaving. I was scared to do it, of course, but I knew if I wanted to wear tank tops and not be talked about I was going to have to do it. The same was true with my legs. Some women shave their legs while others don't and the same is true for underarms. You have to know what you are comfortable with. Hair traps body odors and bacteria, so if you aren't willing to shave it you have to at least keep it clean and dry. There are hair removing lotions, but they take time and can smell pretty bad. With time and experimenting you will figure out what you feel is best for you.

3. **Miscellaneous cracks and crevices**- that would be the belly button, crease between your buttocks, between toes, behind and inside ears. You may think it's not all that important but I'm telling you, these areas can get so nasty smelling when you don't wash them it's unbelievable. When I was little, I knew a girl whose belly button was black. I couldn't understand it, so I asked her about it and she told me that it was because you weren't supposed to wash your belly button. Hey, I figured she knew what she was talking about since she was so much older than me, so...I stopped trying to clean it. Then one day I happened to be playing around, picking at the accumulated dirt and lint, then put my fingers to my nose...WOW! That was one of the worst smells ever! I immediately got a Q-tip and cleaned it out with alcohol. It took a while, but finally it was clean and I never let that happen again. Some belly buttons are deep, those are the ones that need a little extra care and time to get clean. The same smell is created when you don't clean behind your ears and even inside the holes where your ears are pierced. Try it out: take a whiff of your earrings after wearing them in for a while and you will not be happy. Cleaning your earrings will cut down on the dirt that gets caught inside the hole. Clean the inner folds of your ears with a washcloth. Never dig in your ear with a Q tip, it can do some serious damage.

* **A note on perfume**. Perfume is an addition to your natural body odor; it is not to *create* your scent. Your body reacts to the chemicals in perfume; that is why you could wear a certain perfume and it smells one way and your best friend wear it and it smells different. Trial and error will help you find scents that compliment your natural body odor. Put on just enough that you can barely smell it. I typically put it on my wrists then rub my wrists on my neck; this puts just enough on for me. The perfume clings to your body and when your body heat raises the scent of the perfume is released. Drenching yourself in perfume is a sure way to get people to back away from you and it's annoying to other people when your perfume is over powering. If you can smell your perfume really well, then you probably have on too much and it can be rough on those around you especially if they have sensitivities to chemicals or allergies. A little goes a long way for some perfumes. Body sprays are usually less strong than perfume but too much is still too much.

* **Moisturize your body**: use a good lotion to prevent dry skin. Find one that suits your needs as with everything else. If you have a special skin condition, like eczema, you will have to do some experimenting to get what you need or you may have to get one prescribed by your doctor. The lotion you use on your body isn't always good for your face, so be careful.

When I got my period I didn't know what to do. There were so many myths about how to take care your body during that time. I heard things like don't take a bath, take a shower instead, don't take a shower take a bath instead, don't wash down there at all...I was a mess. But I'll tell you this; it is the most important time to keep clean. When you menstruate, your body is cleansing itself internally. All that comes out needs to be washed away as soon as possible! Not cleaning yourself properly during your cycle can lead to problems with your entire reproductive system. Don't risk your health in any way by listening to myths and stories, bathe like you normally bathe and pay special attention to your vagina and the areas that may collect blood.

Pads Vs. Tampons: This is another tricky one. I had no idea that girls were using tampons when I was in school until one day a classmate told me she did. I was horrified! I couldn't imagine putting anything inside my vagina! As I grew older, I understood that there was a huge difference between the two and that it was all a matter of preference. However, I can say that it is important that you use the absorbency that matches your flow. It is very dangerous to use a super tampon if you only flow lightly. Use the lowest absorbency possible and move up only when you find that you have to change frequently. It is never a good idea to sleep in a tampon, but if you have a very heavy flow sometimes you have too. If you get up in the middle of the night you should change it then. There is the possibility that you may forget that you are wearing a tampon if your flow is light and that is very dangerous! If your flow slows down, switch to a pad until your cycle is done. There are warning labels on tampon boxes that you should read. Follow the instructions, don't just do what you think is best or what you've heard other people do. Pads are a little less frightening, you know which ones will do what you need and they are easy to change and easier to know when they need to be changed. Find one that protects you from leaks! It's never fun to have a feminine accident!

4. Feet: Wash and dry your feet well. Use a good scrub on them to keep them from being rough. They are a very abused area, you're walking around on them all day and they are rubbing the insides of your shoes. This rubbing can cause corns and calluses. Sometimes corns and calluses are due to the way your feet grow. Once they are there that doesn't mean they have to be an unsightly addition to your feet. Soak them and rub the built up skin with a pumice stone or foot stone, then make sure you put on the lotion. Putting powder inside your socks is good to keep down the friction and keep your feet dry as well.

5. Face: this is a hard one. Everyone's skin is different. When puberty comes your skin goes through lots of changes. Some of us get pimples, some don't. I didn't break out until I was 27 years old and adult acne is sometimes worse than acne when you are young. If you have acne you will have to experiment to find what works best for you. If it is serious enough, you may have to get help from a doctor. For the most part, keeping your face clean is the best way to prevent the acne. Take time to read the face soaps and washes and see what they claim they do, compare it to what your face is doing. If it's oily, find an oil free wash, if it's dry find a wash that hydrates and moisturizes. Ask around, if you know someone that has nice skin ask them what they use and get the smallest size of that product, in case it doesn't work you haven't wasted a lot of money. Don't be fooled by the prices, just because it's expensive doesn't mean it will work better. My skin was great in high school and all I used was a gentle, glycerin soap with no added medicine. My face went through all kinds of changes over the years and right now I'm back to a gentle foaming cleanser and my skin looks pretty good. It's very important to moisturize no matter what type of skin you have. Find a moisturizer for your skin type just like you did with the cleanser. Most important: drinking water is the best thing you can do for your skin!

6. Hair: So many products, so little time! It can be very difficult to figure out what product is best for your hair sometimes. Like your skin, your hair will change as you age. Your hair is your crowning glory; it's one of the first things people notice about you outside of your face! Don't think that because a style looks good, that it will be good for your hair. Many times the stylist is more interested in giving you what you want and getting paid than making sure your hair is healthy. There seems to be just as many balding women now -a -days as men! Using a lot of chemicals on your hair will lead to problems down the road or possibly losing your hair and not being able to regrow it. I've found that the best thing for my hair has been to use as few products as possible. My brother had beautiful hair and he told me one time to not put ANYTHING on my hair if I wanted it to be healthy. I didn't listen, I was brainwashed by all the commercials and the huge amount of products in the store. I had so many different kinds of products it was crazy! Even with all those products I often still couldn't get my hair to feel and look the way I wanted. Once I stopped using so many things and let my hair rest and breathe I noticed it was a lot healthier. So now I only have about 2 products in the bathroom for my hair. Less money spent, less time stressing over my hair and more space in the bathroom for other things.

7. Nails: your nails and hair are made up of the same stuff. You have to keep them both moisturized and cleaned. Lotions work great to keep your hands moist and keep your cuticles from cracking. One of the most painful and aggravating things is split cuticles! Keep your nails trimmed and filed neatly. Acrylic nails may look good, but they are not good for your nails. Sometimes the salons will take away far too much of your natural nail when putting on acrylics and your nails underneath are left weak and damaged. If you just really want to get it done, try to find a salon that does the nails by hand filing and not with a mechanical file; good luck with this b/c I've only found one in my lifetime. Gel nails are less damaging to your nails but the UV light is damaging to the nail bed as well. You can do your nails at home by simply soaking them in a mild dish detergent, pushing your cuticles back, filing, buffing and moisturizing them, and the same can be done with toenails.

I've devoted a lot of time to this area because I wish someone had given me this kind of advice when I was in junior high or earlier. I had some really embarrassing things happen to me that could have been avoided if I'd known more about my body and how to take care of it. There were books out there that could have taught me things but unfortunately, I didn't know. I'm sure there are some now, and there's plenty of information online. Sometimes there is way too much information and you still can figure out what's best, kind of like my issue with hair care products! If you are confused, try to find someone you feel comfortable talking to and get advice from them. Sadly, I couldn't talk to my family about some of these things, which was another reason I had so many embarrassing things happen to me. But if you have a good relationship with your family then go to them for advice. Choose other resources that you feel comfortable with as well; school nurse, your regular doctor or nurse, a favorite female teacher, your best friends Grandma even!

I feel a female should be like a flower: fresh, soft and lightly fragrant. Your pride in yourself is reflected in the way you take care of yourself. Keeping yourself clean keeps you healthy in many ways.

Things to think about:

- Think of a woman you feel takes good care of her body. What makes you feel she takes good care of herself?
- What does she smell like?

- What does she do that makes her look pretty or feminine?
- Is there anyone that helps you learn about your body and what's best for it? If there is no one then take the time to do your own research and learning, it's one of the best things you can do for yourself! Read the magazines in the store, if you can't buy them, go to the library, and don't be afraid to simply ask another woman what she does to care for her body!
- What things would you like to improve on as far as your body care?
- Is there anything you are confused about as far as what you should be doing to care for your body? Who have you talked to? Don't be afraid to ask questions when the time comes, like in health class or biology class. If you don't feel comfortable asking in front of the class, try to catch the teacher after or before class to ask.

Tech NOooo

I'm not sure what famous person said it but they spoke of a time when technology would take the place of human interaction. So sadly, it seems that the time is coming really soon if it isn't here already. Take a look around while you are out and see how many people are glued to their phones, pads, laptops or other electronic devices. Whole families will sit together and pay no attention to each other, because their eyes are on the devices. Many people would rather text than talk on the phone. Hardly anyone writes letters anymore; okay meaning with paper and pen! Almost everything you need or want to do can be done with a phone, pad, notebook or laptop from buying groceries to looking for a date.

We seem to be losing touch with some simple things in life and I'm not sure how this will affect us in the long run. We are so connected to our devices, but disconnected with the things and people around us. I still like simple things like taking a walk, writing a hand written letter, going on road trips, and most of all, I love to talk to people, face to face. Having a really great conversation is like exercise for the mind and spirit. I don't feel you can truly connect with or know someone unless you communicate in person and can see the expressions on their faces, and hear the tones of their words and watch their body language. In addition, touch is necessary to life! Having someone hug you, hold your hand, pat you on the back when you've done well, hold your head while you cry, these things can't be replaced by a computer. Nor can running through a pile of leaves in the fall, making a snowman or angel or feeling the wind in your face while riding a bike.

I've said it a few times already and I'll say it again, technology has its benefits, I am not saying that it will be the cause of the fall of civilization. I'm just saying that we were put here to live and love together and to connect with people and enjoy one another. It is sad that so many people want to feel connected to the world around them by being on a continual feed with social media, but can't sit down and talk to their grandparents. Even at work people are hanging on to their phones and can barely get what needs to be done completed because they don't want to miss out on something from their phones. I get so mad when I go shopping or out to eat and the person that's supposed to be providing customer service is glued to their phone and acts like it's a chore to help me. Um, they are getting paid to help people, not ignore them. I hate being in public and people are so preoccupied with their phones that they fail to be considerate of others, or see that no one wants to hear their conversation. People that slow down lines in the store because they are looking at the phone rather than getting their wallet out to pay for their items. And the worst is people that are on the phone while driving. Driving is one of the most dangerous things you can do. You are piloting a 1000 pound piece of machinery through the streets and in less than a second you can take a life or lose your own because you were preoccupied with the phone.

How much of the world around you do you pay attention to? Do you even notice what's going on, or do you not care because your phone provides so many different types of entertainment that the world around you seems dull? How often do you actually spend time talking to your family? Does everyone go their separate ways at home and develop their social media relationships more than the relationships with the ones they love? How many times have you had a conflict because you misunderstood what someone was saying; like a text that went wrong, you thought a person meant one thing when they meant something else altogether? These are just questions to think about. If everyone is glued to their devices, what can actually get DONE? And how safe is that? I don't think it would be a very safe world or even interesting world if everyone was more interested in what they can find with technology rather than the world right in front of them.

Have you ever wanted to the attention of someone and couldn't get it because they had their nose in their phone or tablet? I've seen so many parents totally oblivious to what their children were doing because they are looking at their phones. I wonder how many special moments are lost because of this, how many kids hearts are broken because they wanted to share something with their parents and a device distraction kept it from happening.

No matter how cool technology can be, it cannot replace certain aspects of living and certain things we need from each other. You can't smell a flower on a computer screen, although I know someone is working hard right now to be able to make it happen. But why pay to experience something that's free and right outside your door? Technology was created and continues to be created to assist and serve humans, not to replace them or the experiences and interactions between them.

Give yourself the treat of disconnecting. Give your brain the stimulation of natural everyday things; the feel of the sun on your face, tickling a baby, climbing a tree...reading a book, a real one, not Kindle!

It is a blessing to see and experience the world as God made it; don't take it or people for granted. Once they are gone you won't be able to recreate them on a pad. And even if you could create a conversation with an electronic device with a grandparent you loved but has died, it won't be the same as the ones you could have had with them face to face.

Can You Hear Me Now...

- How much time do you spend on your phone?
- Do you find that you lose track of time?
- Do things get missed or forgotten because you were in your phone (homework, chores, and important dates)?
- Have you ever hurt someone's feelings because you were more interested in your phone than spending time with them? Or vice versa...your feelings were hurt by this lack of attention.
- Do you think you could make it through the day without your phone?

- I often think back to the time before cell phones and remember how things were done, how we got from place to place and how we communicated. You may have no idea how to even do this, but it could save your life one day. The more we depend on technology to do things, the more basic skills we lose (like how to get from A to B without GPS). Watch some old movies and see how people use to live! There will come a time when the "old" ways will be needed.

The Devil's Workshop

I'm sure you have probably heard this saying at some point in time: an idle mind is the devil's workshop. If you don't know what that means let me explain. When your mind is idle (not thinking, working on something), then it gives the devil the opportunity to go to work in it. I don't know of anything good the devil could do with anyone or their minds, so this is not something you should be looking forward to or planning for.

When I was little I spent lots of time alone because I was the only child in the house. The only other young person in the house was seven years older than me so we didn't have a whole lot in common. So if I wasn't outside with kids my own age I was in the house doing things I wanted to do. I loved to read, color, draw, make things out of paper, play with dolls, build houses from cards, and lots of other things. I used to get excited when my aunt or my grandmother would run out of thread because I would use the empty wooden spools to make animals and whatever else I could think of. My brother was always fascinated with what I could do with a piece of wax I'd found or some string, and I loved showing off my creations to people or giving them away. But I realized some time ago, that the older I got, the less time I took to do things that I loved to do as a child. I stopped making little creations with things I found, I stopped drawing and painting, I just didn't have the excitement and drive anymore. I never lost my joy of reading and writing, however, and so that was how I spent most of my spare time.

Fortunately, as a kid I didn't allow the devil many opportunities to get busy with my mind. I wasn't interested in some of the destructive things other kids did when they were at home, like smoking, drinking, going on joyrides, shoplifting, vandalizing property, or staying out late partying. These kids didn't have much going on in their minds that would keep them from allowing the devil to drop a destructive idea in and then watching it go to work. They didn't have any hobbies. They may have felt their destructive behavior was a hobby, but a hobby is usually something that's fun and cool in a positive way. Once they found themselves bored they looked for something to do, and unfortunately the invitation to do something negative took root before something good could. Being bored is a scary thing. Feeling like you have nothing to do will drive you near insanity. So when something came along to take them out of that boredom, they ran with it. So you have to be very careful, and take preventative measures to keep yourself from getting bored and having something or someone use it against you.

Many times I hear young ladies complain that they are bored. I ask them what they like to do, and they say, "I don't know". That's the first sign that they are headed for trouble, and often it's what caused a number of young girls to end up in detention facilities. If you don't know what you like, you probably haven't invested any time trying to find out what kinds of things you like. If you like physical education at school, you would probably like it on a sports team of some type. If you like to read you might love being in a book club. If you like to think and try to figure things out, you might love cross word puzzles or jigsaw puzzles. Some people won't even try new things. They see people doing things and say that looks stupid and never give it a shot. It's like when people say they don't like certain foods and you ask if they have ever even eaten them and they say no. Well, how on earth could you not like it if you've never even tried it?!! They haven't tried it because it "looks nasty", or it "smells funny", that's just crazy. I would have never known I liked certain things if I hadn't just jumped in and said, "Can I do that?" I love to sew and would never have known that if my grandmother hadn't asked me one day to thread a needle for her. After that I was hooked. I used to think I would never go snorkeling. I thought it required you being in deep water and that was out because I couldn't swim. And I thought you had to be in the ocean and that meant there were extra dangers, like sharks and whatnot. Silly me, I found out there were other places to go snorkeling than the ocean, that the water didn't have to be deep and that it was awesome! Now I can't wait to do it again. I didn't let fear keep me from going when I had the opportunity. I felt the same way, if not more so, about camping. I thought it was the stupidest thing ever! Why sleep in a tent outside when there's a perfectly good bed in the house, and no bugs or bears and the bathroom is right there. But camping, canoeing and doing confidence courses were a part of the job I took right out of the military. Although I was scared, got frustrated to the point of crying trying to learn how to steer a canoe, was terrified of heights, and couldn't swim, I discovered I loved doing these things once I tried them out! Camping is one of the most liberating experiences ever. And once I conquered my fear of those things I got to teach young ladies how to do them that never had and who were just as scared as I was the first time. I was in my 30s when I even attempted all this stuff, so that saying, "you can't teach and old dog new tricks" is a lie. Younger people are supposed to be more apt to try new things and be unafraid, so what are you waiting for? Don't let the devil set up shop in your idle, bored mind. Discover what you can do and what you like that will keep your mind productively occupied.

For the inexperienced hunter:

- What subjects do you like at school?
- What types of activities after school can be connected with some of the subjects you like? (Hints: art = art club, talking = debate team)
- What about things you're just interested in?
- Do you like animals and the outdoors? There may be things going on in your community or city that you can be involved in. If you like kids, baby- sit. You get to be around kids and get paid. If you like animals, volunteer at the shelter to take care of the animals. If you enjoy the great outdoors, there are camps and summer programs available through churches and community organizations.
- There are probably after school organizations that cater to your age group too. Just look in the phone book or the newspaper.

- Before the Internet, there was this thing called the Library. I believe it still exists! You can find out what's going on all over the place and find a connection to a hobby and borrow some books, CDs, or a DVD at the same time, for FREE! Just don't forget to turn what you borrowed back in on time!

- If you are already a member of a church, most of the time there are programs going on throughout the week for youth, just pay attention during service and listen to the announcements or *read* the program instead of using it for a fan.

The Joneses

Many people live their lives trying to keep up with the Joneses. I have no idea where this saying came from or who the original Joneses were. But it means trying to have the latest and greatest material things. These people want the best things, the newest things and to be one of the first to get them. They want their neighbors, friends, coworkers, whoever, to see that they have these things. They will go into serious debt trying to make sure they have these things. They worry about what other people think about them. They have a set schedule for when they think they should have certain things, and if they don't get these things when they think they should, they feel like failures and work hard to cover up the "failure".

From sixth grade on up I had one of the worst wardrobes in our school, or so I thought. It wasn't because our family was struggling financially; it was because of the way my aunt chose to dress me and where she chose to buy my clothes. I got made fun so much I dreaded going to school at times. Whenever a new style would come out, I could never have it. I would be stuck with whatever clothes my aunt agreed with and I had to see everyone else showing off their new stuff while I had the same stuff the whole school year.

Once I got to college I could pick my own clothes and oh man was I happy. When I finally got to choose what I wanted to wear I felt better about myself and enjoyed being able to express my sense of style. But at the same time, there were things I wanted that I couldn't really afford. So I got my first credit card, that was my plan to get the things I wanted; buy now, pay later. But paying later got to be later, and later and later; I was paying for things I'd bought months earlier. Then my bills started getting paid later and later and later. I had a number of cards and they were all to their maximum limit! I would pay the minimum amount required and the balance would just remain the same or get worse due to the interest on them. It was terrible, and it took a long time for me to learn a very valuable lesson. Had I focused more on the fact that I was blessed to just have clothes that were clean and that fit I would have saved a lot of money and not damaged my credit history either.

I went through another bit of drama when I graduated from college. I thought I would just walk right into a great job since I had a degree. I thought I'd be able to buy a house, get that nice new car and live like I always dreamed. That was so not the case. There were thousands of other students I had to compete with, I didn't even know what I really wanted to do, and I had all those stupid bills! After a while I started feeling like a first class failure. I saw people I'd graduated from high school with driving nice cars, living on their own, wearing nice clothes, living the life I wanted to live! I sank into a depression and stayed there for a while. I wasn't able to go anywhere without comparing what I had to what other people had. All around me were the images society wanted me to believe was the American dream; in magazines, TV, movies, videos and billboards. I was obsessed with not being able to keep up with the Joneses! I was a miserable mess.

Then one day I talked to a guy I'd gone to high school with and I whined and complained about how jacked up my life was and how I hadn't accomplished nearly enough that showed I was "successful". Well, he started rattling off the names of people we'd gone to school with that I thought were the coolest ones. They were kids I didn't hang out with because I was not in their league as far as my clothes, my personality, and the things I did outside of school. It turned out a number of them were dead. Some of them were fighting drug addictions. Most of them had none of the things they had when we were in school. This same old classmate also started listing the number of accomplishments I'd had, things I never even considered to be accomplishments. After a while of listening to him I kind of felt like an idiot for not having seen all the things I'd done that many people never get a chance to do! I had taken my own blessings for granted and allowed myself to fall into the deceptive trap created when you compare yourself to others.

Many times you will see people and wish you had their lifestyle. But you don't really know what kind of lives these people have. They may be in debt up to their ears, living paycheck to paycheck. They may be driving a nice car and living in a house that will fall if a good storm hits. Never assume that someone has a life better than yours from his or her outward appearances.

Character is priceless. Some of the greatest people you will ever meet may have very little materially or financially. Never underestimate the person inside you or the things you've done either. A sermon I heard once was titled, "God's not finished with me yet." The pastor explained that who you are now is not the person you will always be, in your eyes or God's.

Once I got my mind right and understood that life was not about how much you could accumulate materially, or being able to keep up with the latest fashions I was free in a way I'd never been. I was able to just live my life, accept where I was in life and know that being happy comes from things that have nothing to do with money. Don't get me wrong either, I'm not saying that you need to be poor financially in order to have good character, or deprive yourself of nice things in order to be humble. I'm saying that there are some things money, nice clothes and a Mercedes can't get you. And as one of my supervisors used to say, "You can't take it with you"; meaning once this life is over, all that bling gets left behind. When you spend your time comparing your life to other people it doesn't leave much time for you to work on your life and make it into one that you want or appreciate.

Live a life that you wouldn't want to trade anyone for. Make plans to do the things you want to do. Write them out, pray, and have faith that God will set you up for success. My grandmother told me that there was always room at the top, so you can go as high as you want to regardless of what anyone else may have to say about it. Design your life just like you would draw a picture; create the life you want to live. Talk to successful people who are happy with their lives, have good foundations, and live healthy lifestyles; meaning they treat people well, and do things the right and legal way. Once you take the chance to live the best life you can you can't blame anyone else for the things you feel you don't have. Do the best with what you have now until you can do better. If you can't dress the way you want now, appreciate that you at least have that much and take care of it like it was the stuff you really want and in time you will have the things you want and know how to make them last longer.

Some of the most successful people today started out with very little. They didn't allow themselves to feel sorry for themselves; they made a plan to have more, do more and stuck with it. They didn't have some secret recipe for success, they made it up along the way or borrowed from someone else. So start your own cookbook for your life!

One life to live

- Do you find yourself wondering what it would be like to be in someone else's shoes?

- Who do you want to be like or have a life like and why? Do you know these people personally?
- Do you get upset when you see what other people have that you don't have? Do you feel it's not fair in some ways that they have it and you don't?
- Do you go through magazines daydreaming about what it would be like to have what you see if you don't already have the things? Do you have a plan to somehow get some of the things you see on TV or in magazines that you'd love to have?

- Do you feel unsatisfied with the person you are based on what you feel about some of the people around you? Do you feel you need to look a certain way or have certain things in order to appear to the world that you are successful?

- What kind of life do you feel you need to feel successful and complete? What is your plan to create that life, and is it a life people could look to as an example for themselves?

Try this...

Read an autobiography of someone famous. Find out how they became who they are.

The Process

It's never easy dealing with the death of a loved one whether it's expected, unexpected or even happened when you were too young to understand it. My parents died when I was three and I am still dealing with it 40 plus years later. Most recently my brother died, in 2013 and I had to make all the arrangements myself which made things ten times harder.

One of the best things I was told when my brother died was that grieving is a process. For whatever reason, this made me feel better because it allowed me to let go of the stress of feeling I had to deal with it all at one time. And it helped me understand why I felt different ways at different times. I wasn't told this about my parent's deaths because I was a child. But the thing is, I still have had to go through some of the same steps of grieving even though it's been such a long time since they passed away. There are days when I can think about my family and I'm fine, I might laugh about something I remember about them or just have passing thoughts about them in general. Then there are days when suddenly I recall something they did or someone says something that reminds me of them and I'm in tears. Either way, I understand that this is all normal and I can expect that this may continue to happen for many years to come.

I have had help with this process. I have been fortunate to have some good friends and family members that helped me get through times when I've felt really sad, lonely and even depressed. I've also had some professional help. All throughout this book I've advised seeking assistance from others when things are hard. That help can come in many forms. The point is you don't have to struggle all by yourself. There are people that are willing to help you by doing things you ask and sometimes people will offer help when you least expect it. Sometimes it's when you are dealing with something really overwhelming that the help of others is most valuable. At those times people can surprise you with the wisdom they share. They may never have told you that they lost a loved one, but seeing you hurt gives them strength and motivation to share their story. Even if this person is not someone you would normally talk to or spend time with, allow them to be there for you if they choose and it feels helpful to you.

We all deal with death and grieving differently. If an entire family is dealing with a death things can be very chaotic and unpleasant. There may be clashes that erupt simply because emotions are running high. Things may be said that are hurtful and things may happen that are totally out of character for some. For instance the person that doesn't smoke may start smoking, the person that doesn't drink may drink. You may experience feelings and thoughts you never have before.

Sometimes people will attempt to help you in some way and it only makes things harder for you. At these times it is okay to tell them that you appreciate their willingness to help but that you just aren't up to it at that point. Hopefully they will respect your wishes and hold their tongues.

In addition to people, there are other resources for helping you get through this challenging time. There are a number of books available and for all age ranges. And of course there are always on line resources, like chatting with a grief counselor or websites with valuable information that you can read and calendars for groups that meet to talk about their experiences and gather support from one another. Take the time to think about which of the resources you feel may fit your needs.

There will be times that you simply can't be around others or talk; and that's okay too. Take the time you need alone and maybe in that time write down your feelings and thoughts. Keeping a journal is like having a very special counselor: yourself. There will be things you need to sort out and examine that maybe no one else can understand. I have journaled since I was probably old enough to put sentences together correctly. It is one of the best support systems I have for myself. There have been times when I needed to use my journal to communicate some things I didn't want to express to anyone else. Writing helps me to clear my mind and often allows me to see things differently, answer questions and figure things out. I can also go back to my journals when I need to see how I dealt with something that comes up again.

There are no certain and specific, right and wrong ways to deal with death. There are healthy and unhealthy ways however. If you know you are doing something that is unhealthy during this time, you have to stop. You can't use your sadness or anger as an excuse to do things you normally wouldn't do and that you are AWARE you are doing. Sometimes it takes someone else telling us we are doing something unhealthy. So if you are getting warnings and being told you are out of control, you probably are, so slow your roll. You may very well be angry during this time, but you cannot abuse others as a way of dealing with this anger.

Time is one of the best healers of wounds like this one. Know that it will take time to get through this and remember that you don't have to do it alone. I know sometimes it's hard to hear but God knows what He is doing. You may be mad at God, He will actually understand. And He is there none the less so talk to Him, whatever emotions you may be experiencing He is the ever present listening ear, comforter and counselor.

Saying Goodbye

- Are you trying to process emotions related to the death of a loved one? How long have you been doing this?
- What has been the hardest part of this process for you?
- Who has made things a little better? Who has made things harder?
- How has your family reacted to this process? What changes have you noticed in them, good and bad?
- What emotion is greater for you now and how are you dealing with it?
- Are you mad at God? Have you told Him?
- If you didn't get to say goodbye do you feel you still can't? why or why not?

Things that may seem strange but still help...
- Writing letters to the ones you lost. I did it and I felt so much better!
- Talk to them as if they are still there. Hearing yourself say what's on your mind out loud can help release a lot of things you feel are heavy.
- Put together a project for them. I made a collage of all the pictures I had of my brother and wrote a letter to him on the back of it. It was the greatest thing that helped me get through his burial.
- Use whatever talent you may possess to help you move forward: writing, crafts, poems, painting...whatever! There are no limits to what you can do and it may just help others who are struggling as well.

The Wrong Prince

So you have a boyfriend. You believe he is just perfect in every way and you love the attention he gives you. You are willing to do whatever he needs to keep him because you think that's what you are supposed to do right? Well, it is to a point. In order for a relationship to be healthy, there has to be mutual respect, kindness and consideration. The thing is, if you don't have a healthy sense of self-esteem you will be the one that does all the giving and doing and your boyfriend may just take advantage of this.

When you decide to be in a relationship with someone, there should be a balance. You can't be the only one that does the giving; meaning, giving your time, making phone calls, exchanging gifts, whatever. You have to value yourself and be comfortable with your own company first and foremost. If you feel you have to have other people in your life in order to feel loved or needed this can blind you to people that will take advantage of your kindness and giving nature. Unfortunately there are people that prey on others that feel lonely, unhappy, unpretty, unpopular etc. They latch onto this person and use them to get things they want. Sometimes you end up in a situation like this before you realize what's going on! You are so happy to have someone giving you attention that you feel it's okay to give them everything you have. But this is not what a healthy relationship is.

Sometimes we know in our hearts that the guy we want is not the right one for us but we think that we can get him to change. This has got to be one of the top five reasons relationships don't work, for teenagers as well as adults. As women, most of us have this thing in our heads that we can make any situation better, we want to be able to fix everything and make it all better. So when we find a guy we like that's struggling with something (his homework, his teachers, his parents, his siblings, his skateboard, whatever) we want to step in there and take it all away. We think if we just love him enough we will be all he needs to be happy, and in turn he will love us the same way. WRONG, WRONG, EXTRA WRONG! Whoever this guy is when you meet him, that's who he is. He will more than likely not change much. He may mature, even change his feelings about some things in time, but to expect an overall turnaround into someone who will love and respect you is an absolute waste of time. If he wasn't respectful from the start don't expect him to suddenly become respectful just because you have given him everything he's asked for and then some. Never, ever, ever go into a relationship with the intent of being that person's personal savior. He may only use you for all the great things you do and then dump you. In the process he may have several other girls just like you on the side.

Unfortunately sometimes we don't have the best role models for what is best for us. Some research shows that girls tend to use the relationship they had with their fathers or whatever male they had the most relationship with at home as a guide for what they want in a relationship with a male they are interested in. If you didn't have a good male role model in your life you may not have much guidance as to how a man is supposed to treat a woman. If the relationship between your parents or whoever you grew up with was not a very healthy one, you may even copy some of the bad things that you saw simply because it's what you saw and experienced. And on the other hand, if the relationship was a healthy one you may tend to expect the same things from the guy you are interested in. There are lots of factors involved in who we end up attracted to and what kind of relationships we build over our lifetimes

When I first realized I liked boys and wanted their attention I started giving them things. I thought if I bought or gave them things they might like, they had to like me and want to be with me. I don't even know where I got the idea from but I must have thought I didn't have much to offer, so I had to have something nice to give them. I told you about "Billy" and the wristbands. I felt so stupid when he gave them back and said, "I don't even know you." I never even thought to just introduce myself to him and let him find out what kind of person I was, see if he was even interested in getting to know me. But did I learn my lesson then? NOPE. I kept up the fantasy that one day I would come up with the right gift for the right guy and we would live happily ever after. It has taken a long time for me to stop repeating this pattern. I had good male role models in my family that I didn't ask about romantic relationships, nor did I recognize they their behaviors should have been those I looked for in a boyfriend. My Grandfather was one of those role models. He treated my Grandmother with respect and love. I saw him to things for her that no other men in my family were doing for their wives. Although the uncle l lived with gave me some great advice about how to deal with romance and boyfriends, it wasn't until I was almost out of high school. And unfortunately because he was the male I saw most often, it was his behaviors I sought in my partners. Although he gave me good advice, he did not demonstrate consistently healthy and loving behaviors towards my aunt.

There are some things you give away that you can't just get back or simply get over because they are not material, but emotional and even physical. Over the years I learned that being super nice to guys only makes them run the other way. They can oftentimes look at you and tell that you will bend over backwards to have them in your life. Some guys see this as a game to be played and they will run through you like bag of potato chips. Other guys see this as a huge turn off and will simply ignore you if you try to overwhelm them with your generosity. I had a cousin that always had a boyfriend or some guy chasing her. She was so mean to the boys that called her yet they would continue to blow the phone up trying to get her to give them a chance. I didn't learn even in junior high that she was making them work for her attention. She was the prize they had to win. Me, on the other hand, thought the guys were the prize and ran around like an idiot trying to win their affections.

Sometimes we do things and don't even realize we are doing them until years later. It took me a very long time to see how unhealthy my perspective was on how I chose my boyfriends. That meant I was hurt time and time again because I kept repeating the same mistakes. I wasn't mature enough to know to take a look at my patterns of behavior and think about the kind of males I was being attracted to. One more reason I am writing this book. I want you to have a chance to learn about yourself and recognize your own behaviors that may cause you to repeat the same mistakes. There is no reason ever to stay in a relationship that causes stress, hurt and confusion. Love is not supposed to hurt. Yes, of course, in relationships there will be up and downs. But when the downs outnumber the ups, it's time to go. And when you go, only look back at the experience as a lesson; what was good, what was bad, and why. Then do your best to not repeat any part that you know in your heart made it unhealthy.

If you find yourself in any of these situations you may need to re-evaluate your relationship:
~ you see him with other females who are hanging all on him and he does nothing to get them off

~ he only calls you when he needs something

~ you spend more money on him than yourself

~ he makes you feel guilty when you ask him about something he's done

~ he goes all out to clear up a situation when he knows he's been caught: giving you gifts, telling you he won't ever do it again...then he does it again.

~ you find all kinds of stuff given to him from other females and he says, "they are just friends"

~you see another girl with a gift that you know you gave him

~he embarrasses you in front of people and claims he was only kidding when you confront him about it

~he acts like you aren't even there when his friends come around

~he doesn't introduce you to people when you are out together and he runs into someone he knows

You must allow people to earn your love and respect; you can't just give yourself away to people with the hope that they will return your feelings. If you give and give and never get back, that's not their problem, it's yours. If you let one person disrespect you and play with your emotions, others will see that they can treat you the same way and they will also attempt it. Protect yourself, know that you are worthy of the best and never accept anything less when it comes to how people treat you.

In essence you can't blame him for what he does when you knew in your heart that he wasn't doing the right things in the first place. Finding someone that truly cares for you may not happen when you want it to but there is no need to accept just anyone because you are afraid you won't find someone else. Very few people find true love at your age and far too many stay with the wrong person for the wrong reasons. Let God send you your prince, don't go kissing a bunch of frogs trying to find him.

And the verdict is...

- What kind of guy do you want as a boyfriend? Make a list of all the things that are important to you.
- Do you do things to try to get a guy's attention? If so, what do you do and has it worked in the past. How did you feel afterwards?
- If you have a boyfriend now, does he treat you like you want to be treated? If not, what have you done about it? Why do you stay with him?
- How important is it to you to have a boyfriend? Do you worry about what other people will say?
- Are you spending a lot of time doing things to make him happy and losing track of other responsibilities?
- Who is putting forth the most effort to get the relationship to work? Is it equal or lopsided?
- Are you chasing a guy down who isn't paying you any attention? What are expecting to get out of this?
- If there is a guy interested in you, what kind of things does he do to make you feel he respects you? Is he consistent with these things or does he only do them to get something in return?

You must first learn to love yourself before you can truly learn how to love another.

To Thy Own Self Be True

Someone told me this a while ago: To thy own self be true. It came at a very important time in my life. I was running around trying really hard to please people but doing nothing to help myself. I didn't know who I was or where I fit into the world and generally had a pretty poor, self- pitying attitude. I felt like the world owed me something because of all the hard times I'd gone through. But instead of looking into myself to see where things went wrong I tried to do things to make people happy or to like me when I didn't even like myself enough to know **how** to be happy. Everyone needs to know how to appreciate one's self, regardless of what people may say about you. Now, don't get this wrong! I don't mean to get crazy with this and think you can do whatever and say whatever you want and as long as you're fine with it it's okay.

You need some examples right? Okay…I've always admired people that follow their dreams, even when it seems near impossible to achieve them.

So, someone tells a guy he's too short to play pro basketball, he's crazy to even consider it. He says to himself, "Forget that!" practices and plays his hardest and ends up in the NBA as one of the shortest but most powerful and dynamic players. A young woman struggles in math but wants to be a doctor. Her parents tell her to pick something easier for her to manage or that she's good at. She says "No Way", gets all the help she can find, studies her hardest, finds new ways to learn and understand math, and eventually graduates from medical school years later. And these are just a couple of examples of being true to oneself.

My grandmother and I were sitting on the porch one day and she asked what I wanted to be when I got older she said "There's always room at the top." She didn't have to say anything else. I knew she meant that no matter what I wanted to do, I could succeed in it because there was no limit to success; everyone and anyone could have it. There is no set number of people that are allowed to succeed and once that number is reached, everyone else needs to just give up their dreams or desires.

Some of my family were not too keen on my decision to become a youth counselor. They said I didn't know anything about kids and suggested I choose something else that paid more money and that sounded better in case someone asked, "So, what do you do?" You know what I said right? Yep...Forget that! And I took the job. Yes, it was one of the hardest things I've ever done, but I loved it and got lots of compliments from my boss, received achievement awards, and had a number of the girls tell me I'd helped them change their lives. I even got to be on TV because one particular young lady who'd been sent to the program chose me to be there with her when she went back for a follow-up story about her success! Ha! Pretty good for someone that didn't know jack about kids, huh?

An English teacher I had in high school once showed the class a video of a man who had only parts of his legs, no arms and severely deforming burns over most of his body. He was one of only a few men whose wives stood by him and loved him regardless of his appearance after he returned from a military combat zone. Well, this same man became a concert pianist by using his toes and other parts of his body. It was an awesome video and I've never forgotten that video or the wisdom of my teacher for sharing it with us.

So, listen to your heart sometimes, not just your head. Sometimes people will cram lots of doubts into your head and if you let them, those doubts will slide into your heart and create fear. Sometimes on your own you will create a bunch of doubts about what you can and can't do. I've lost and wasted a lot of time being scared to just try. God only knows what kinds of successes I've let pass me by. There's a saying: nothing beats a failure like a try. So the only real failure there is, is **not** trying. So, shake those haters off: friends, family, anyone who tries to tell you your dream or goal is too hard or simply not possible.

It's really nice to have someone around you that's beat the odds and done something even they didn't think they could do. These types of people are not hard to find, you'd be surprised; they are all around you. Don't be afraid to just ask someone about their lives, then listen to their testimonies and learn from them. Have some faith in you and just do it.

Think on it:
- What are your dreams?
- Has someone said it's too hard for you?
- What keeps you from trying if you haven't been?
- What do you have to lose if it doesn't turn out the way you want it to?
- If it doesn't work out, what makes you think you couldn't recover and just try again?
- Who is least supportive of your dreams? Why do you think they aren't supportive? Why does their opinion count?
- Who is most supportive of your dreams? Why do you think they support you? Why does their opinion count?
- If you are in the process of working towards your goal, what keeps you going; motivates you?

Challenge: think of something relatively simple that you've always wanted to do but were scared or just procrastinated with, and do it and write down how it made you feel, even if it didn't work out, how did it feel just to *try?*

Watch Your Mouth!

Oh the almighty power of the word. Sticks and stones may break my bones, but words will put me in my grave. Yeah, I know that's not how the saying really goes, but it's the truth. How many times have you said something and wished you'd just kept your mouth shut? And how many times has someone said something about you and you wonder, what the...? Where did they get that?

One day I heard a woman talking about her grandchild. She was saying how troublesome the little girl was in daycare and how she interacted with the other kids in her class. She made a comment saying that the little girl would likely be the one in the family would end up in jail or in some other really bad situations once she was older. She was talking about her like she wasn't there, but she was in the same room and her older sister was listening too. The little girl's mother made similar comments about her, so I knew this was regular talk for them. The whole scene really upset me because that little girl will probably end up doing some of the negative things her family suggested because they put it into words and seem to be waiting for it to happen. So what's to stop her? And if her family complains about it once it does happen, guess what she can say, "Well, you guys SAID I would do it!"

One of my pastors spent a lot of time letting our church know that many times we had set ourselves up for failure by speaking things into being. Meaning, if you are always telling yourself that you can't finish school because you aren't smart enough, you probably won't finish. If you say you can't resist drugs because you aren't strong enough, you probably won't. And if someone is always telling you that you are worthless and stupid, you may eventually come to believe it and say it yourself and BAM, you've allowed yourself to be set up for failure with thoughts and words alone. When you speak it, you probably believe it and therefore you give it life. You have to choose what you want to speak and what you want to bring to life.

Like many other young ladies, I had some rough times when I was growing up; I've been called names, talked about, and been made fun of. Although I never spoke what people said aloud to myself I spoke them on the inside and the words damaged my feelings about myself; my self-esteem, and self- confidence. On the flip side, I had lots of people that told me what a great student I was, what a wonderful person I was, how talented I was, how smart I was. Some of the same people that were verbally abusive, praised me for some of my achievements. So I had all those mixed bits of information floating around inside. I wasn't sure what I was: trifling and ugly, or a talented and beautiful young lady. So every time I failed at something, those blaring, hurtful comments came up and left me depressed. And if I succeeded at something, I'd feel great about it, but underneath it all I questioned if it was really a success or just some quick luck for me.

The things said to me as I was developing into a young woman were like blocks I used to build my inner person. Some blocks were weak and crumbling (the negative stuff), and other blocks were strong and supporting (good stuff). As I became an adult those weak blocks kept me from having a solid, confident form. I was easily offended, extremely defensive, and had huge chip on my shoulder thinking people should feel sorry for me and help me all the time. Fortunately I realized one day that I needed some serious remodeling! I had to take out those weak blocks and reform myself from the inside out. As I removed those blocks, people around me began to notice; I was more confident because I felt stronger *inside*. I refused to continue being seen as a broken down, pitiful structure. And I had to understand that once I took those blocks out I needed to stop blaming the people and situations that created them in the past. I had to put in new blocks of my own and take responsibility for the building I was creating. I knew the negative things that were said to me in the past weren't true and once I told myself this, I had to make it so, believe it, and live it. I still struggle at times when I feel attacked by people's words or behavior toward me. But I make myself stop, regroup, see the negative things for what they are and kick it all to the curb. I don't ever want to be a condemned building again. I had to actually say aloud: I am worthy, I am good, I am smart, I deserve good things, I will succeed, I can do it! Saying them, speaking them into existence is powerful!

Many people can't get past living what others have spoken into their lives. They soak up every negative thing said about them, holding on to the words like they are clothing and they wear them all their lives. Even when people try to help them, show them a different way of living, they refuse to get rid of those old clothes and try some new ones. They get so used to the old ones that they don't feel anything else will fit them. I'm using a lot of symbolism here but I think you know what I'm trying to say. There are people that get so used to a way of life that they are not willing to try to change it into something new. If this reminds you of you, you need to start getting control of it right now!

One thing you need to do if you find yourself putting yourself down because of what other people say is to get around some people that bring out the best in you. Seek out environments that are supportive, positive, and nurturing. If the people you surround yourself with use you as the punching bag, embarrass you to get their kicks, or worse, you need to make some changes. How do you want your development into a woman to be dictated: by people who find all your weaknesses, flaws and handicaps, and broadcast them to make themselves feel better, or by your own collection of positive experiences, supportive interactions and knowledge of your best qualities? Will you let the sticks and stones break your bones, or will you surprise the people that threw them by using them to build yourself up where you are weak?

There is power in words. God SPOKE and things were created. You have the same powers. You can choose what is spoken into your life regardless of what others say. Choose your words wisely and for your benefit.

Speak Life:
- What kind of building would you compare yourself to, one that needs total reconstruction...one that needs some repairs... one that is in pretty good condition?
- What things do you feel make you who you are right now?
- What kind of woman do you want to be? What do you think will help you create that woman? What kind of people do you model yourself after?
- How do other people's comments about you affect you?
- What do YOU say about YOU? What good things do you speak into your own life?
- What things in your life do you feel keep you from being the kind of person you want to be? Can you change any of them? If you can't, what do you think you could do to get around them?
- What things are you pleased with about yourself? What kinds of things do you think helped you develop the things you love about yourself?

Project: Draw a picture of the kind of building or structure you feel represents yourself now. Then draw a picture of the kind of structure you want to be. Be creative, put labels on the things that are roken, give your building a name, put a neighborhood around it to show what things are around you now and what things you would like to be around you in the future.

What's wrong with a virgin?

I had a friend in college who asked me if she should have sex. I was like whoa, she's asking my opinion on something this important? Her father was a pastor, yet she came to me for advice! I couldn't mess this up! I had to give her the best advice regardless of what I was doing personally. So I told her that she needed to make absolutely sure that the person she had sex with was worthy. She needed to know that afterwards he would respect her and love her the same way she respected and loved him. She needed to know that she would not be upset with herself afterwards, feeling anything less than the beautiful young woman that she was before. If these things weren't possible, then she needed to continue to wait. And remember...we were in **college**.

With all the junk that's on T.V., radio, movies, advertisements...I could go on and on...you'd think it was simply okay to have sex. Sex is used to sell just about everything, to influence minds, and even in past times to wage wars. So what's the big deal? Why not just do it and enjoy it? Well, because it's not as easy as it seems. Most females are programmed in some way to associate sexual intercourse with a meaningful event; most often love. We fall in love with our boyfriends and feel like we need to give him this "gift". You think about doing it for a number of reasons: he loves you and deserves it, he will stay with you if I do it, he says he needs it, if you don't do it someone else will and he will like them more. It's hard to detach the emotional feelings from the physical feelings when it comes to sex. Your body may say let's get this party started, but what does your mind tell you.

So my question is...what's wrong with a virgin. Answer: Absolutely nothing. If there were a pill that could let you experience the aftermath of having sex I would mass produce it and give it away free to every young girl myself. And I'm not talking about just the physical after-math, I'm talking about the WHOLE emotional deal: the confusion, the stomach flutters, the anger, the shame, the fear. When you are a virgin you have a power that only last as long as your virginity does. That power allows you to see who really wants to be with you because of YOU and who just wants to have your gift. If a young man wants to love you, he can love you in a million different ways without having to "make love" to you. Do you really feel that you are ready to handle the emotional stress that comes with losing your virginity? How do you handle getting a "D" on a test you studied long and hard for? How do you handle it when you are promised something from someone you care for and then they let you down? What about when your favorite sandwich is no longer on the menu at one of your favorite restaurants? These crises are nothing compared to the stress of having shared your body with another.

 Beware of the friend who claims to have done it and has all the juicy details! She could be lying. Yes, lying. She wants you to think that she is a real live WOMAN and has done something great that you in turn should follow or be jealous of because she has a knowledge that you don't. She thinks it will bring her respect and a sense of admiration from the virgins she knows. Don't believe the hype. Sometimes you will know who really did it from the emotional trauma they seem to carry. You can see this trauma without even having to be told the circumstances, it will be almost written on their faces. Other times you can see it in their bellies because they created a new "gift", meaning a baby.

 Recently there was an article in the paper about kids and their perception of what sex really is. It was shocking because it was not the same as it was even when I was young. Some young people feel that there are things that aren't considered "real" sex, like oral sex for example. They feel like it's no big deal since they didn't have intercourse. BUT, although you can't get pregnant from oral sex, it's still SEX. You are doing something very intimate with your sexual organs for the sole purpose of pleasure. You might ask, "Is kissing sex too?" Well, your mouth isn't always a sexual part of the body, you need it for other stuff. But once you change its function, you change the emotions attached to it. You get a different kind of pleasure from eating than you do kissing.

With sex there are risks: DISEASE. All the pleasure in the world is not worth dealing with a sexually transmitted disease. They are painful, contagious, and some are not curable. AIDS isn't the only thing you should be worried about when it comes to sex; there are a load of other ones that can devastate your life as well: herpes, syphilis, gonorrhea, genital warts, and many others. Take some time to research the diseases associated with sex and how they are contracted and the information may give you plenty of reasons to wait. Many times people jump into things without giving any serious thought to the consequences of the action. Sex is definitely something you want to look at from ALL angles. Really understand what you are about to get yourself into before going ahead with any plans. It's easy to get out of a bad purchase, just take it back to the store. But once you've had sex, you can't just take it back, or go back or erase any of it. It's a onetime deal and that one time can lead to consequences you deal with for the rest of your life and in more bad ways than good if you choose to do it while you are still so very young.

Resisting the temptation to have sex is probably one of the hardest things in life to do because it is made into such a big deal and thrown in our faces every way possible. But it is easier to resist something you've never had than to get a taste of it, find that you really enjoy it, and *then* try to stop. Sex is a desire, a want, **not a need**. It doesn't keep you alive, but it can kill you. If some guy says he NEEDS it from you, it's just a lie to make you feel obligated. So keep the doors shut for now and you won't have to worry about getting rid of things you didn't intent to invite.

Inside the Control Tower

- You can decide to remain a virgin for as long as you choose? Yes or no.
- You don't have to do what other people do in regards to sex? Yes or no.
- There is power in choosing not to have sex? Yes or no.
- There are adults who have never had sex? Yes or No.
- Sex is the most important thing in the world? Yes or No.
- There are pros and cons to having sex, benefits and risks? Yes or No.
- Take time to think about all these questions and even do some research of your own to get some of the answers. My goal is to get you to really think about sex on a number of different levels and determine how you feel about it now and how it may affect you later in life, either before or after you've made the choice to have sex.

Who Are These People?

If you are an only child at home, this chapter may not be of any benefit to you. But you can read it anyway just to see what others have to deal with.

Okay, you've got brothers, sisters, step-brothers, step-sisters, cousins, foster siblings, whatever, all living in the same house. Do you all get along? How many fights break out per week? Are they settled quickly or is there always a hostile environment when you all are home at the same time?

There are so many things that go on in a household where there are multiple young people. Someone's upset that they don't get as much attention as someone else. Someone gets treated better. Someone gets someone else in trouble all the time. Someone lies on someone. Someone stole something from someone. Someone's wearing someone else's clothes, listening to their CDs, borrowing without asking, tattling, breaking something... the list goes on and on.

Sometimes the things that happen between young people in the house they grow up in affects their lives far after they have moved out of the house. Sometimes the tensions and fights are so horrible, healing never takes place and relationships are never mended.

Sometimes things are bad but never so much that bonds are broken. Some siblings grow up together and are close throughout life. It's all just how the cards play themselves out.

So what are you to do when you have these crazy, tension-filled experiences with the young folks you live with? This is a tough one because of the number of reasons behind the stress. I can't pretend to have the answers to every situation you may endure. I surely didn't have any answers for myself, or any ways to avoid the things that happened at my house sometimes. I did find friends that I got along with and spent time with them as much as I could. I did involve myself in the things I liked to do as much as I could. I did get involved with things at school that I enjoyed. I kept a journal that I wrote my feeling in when there was no way I could talk to anyone at home. I talked to my brother about it when I could. He and I didn't live in the same house, he lived with my Grandparents. But we had a special bond and I could always trust him to protect me and listen to me, even if he did torture me sometimes (tickling me, gluing my fingers together, tearing up my dolls...you know, regular big brother type stuff).

You won't always get along with your siblings, you're not supposed to, that's just life. But one thing you have to know and practice is that just because they may treat you in a way you don't feel is fair or kind, it doesn't mean you are supposed to return that same treatment. Paying them back for things they've done can back fire on you. If you take matters into your own hands all the time, it can turn out far worse than you know. Yes you are supposed to defend yourself when you are wronged, but you have to choose your battles wisely. Every disagreement isn't worth a whole lot of working out. Some things are better off left alone and forgotten.

If you find yourself being the object for routine injustices with your siblings, letting them know they are getting to you can be your worst enemy. Kids can be awfully mean to one another and when they see they can get your goat, it makes the game more fun to them. Letting your emotions get the best of you will make a bad situation worse. Learn how to thicken your skin (meaning, not just let any and everything get to you) and when you feel an attack coming on, prepare to be like a duck and let things just roll off your back. Know that sometimes these attacks are not always meant to hurt you.

With all this said, you yourself might be the tormentor in the house. You may be stressing out your siblings by making fun of them, roughing them up, getting them in trouble for your messes. If you are the tormentor, I suggest you get your act together because if you treat your family that way, how do you treat others? Don't think that you won't ever run into someone that's not so easy a target?

Living within a family is an adventure. Sometimes you can control your adventure and sometimes you can't. Do your best to not be the one that causes the problems. Living in a family is an exercise in a number of things; patience, love, kindness, problem solving, understanding, sharing…and it never stops. How you relate to your family can become the way you choose to relate to everyone else. You continue to discover ways new ways to love and learn as you get older. Hopefully you make the best choices so that the memories you have of growing up in your family can be healthy and productive ones that you can use when you have a family of your own.

A Family Affair
- What kinds of problems are constant in your home? Are they problems that can be solved by your behavior or choices?
- Do you feel you have any control over the amount of conflict in your home? If not why?
- What are some good things about your family?
- What kinds of things go on at your home that you would like to carry on to a family that you might have in the future?
- What is your idea of the perfect family?

- How do you get along with the other children in the house if there are any? What things would you change about your relationship with them? If you are close to them, what makes those bonds strong? If your relations with them is strained, what do you think causes the strain and are you willing to try to work it out?

Who Do You Love

When I say who, I'm really asking about you. This is one of the most important questions ever because it determines a majority of the decisions you make throughout your life. Do you love you? I mean really LOVE? Can you look in the mirror and smile at yourself, walk down the street unafraid of what people may say about you. Can you put yourself first instead of always trying to please someone else? I'm not talking about being a selfish, inconsiderate person. I'm saying you love yourself enough not to run yourself in the ground trying to please others and get them to like you.

I've mentioned that throughout my school years I didn't hang out with any one group in particular. I was kind of a loner. I did most stuff by myself, and didn't feel very comfortable trying to be a part of groups because it seemed I was an easy target for teasing. I did, however, do things to make friends and to get people to like me. I was, and still am when I put an honest effort into it, an excellent artist. I was one of the best art students in my middle school. My peers knew this so I tried to use it to my advantage. I would draw pictures and give them away. I enjoyed the attention they gave me when they wanted me to make something for them. I was also a clown. I would do just about anything to get a laugh and often got into trouble for my foolishness. I spent plenty of class time out in the hallways since my teachers would put me out. But none of these things helped me form lasting friendships with anyone in school. In high school I toned down my foolishness because I was more afraid of the consequences of getting in trouble. I kind of floated from one person to the next, getting to know a few people and spending time with them, then finding that we didn't have enough in common to bond. The people I probably would have bonded best with I avoided because they were outsiders, nerds and unknowns like I was. I missed out on making some real friends because I was shallow and afraid. Once I got to college I started clowning again to make friends and I almost got kicked out my first few months there because of it. I was terrified! Fortunately, I made it through the incident and after some soul searching and pretty humiliating situations, I realized I needed to get my act together and do something that required some real discipline- I went into the military. Now, that's a whole different story, so I'll stick to the point of loving myself for now.

It wasn't until I was in my mid-twenties that I really started to look deeply into myself and see what I was made of, what made me tick. I thought about how my personality was formed, what I liked and disliked and why, who I liked and disliked, what was most important to me, why I chose to dress the way I did, who my friends were and who had betrayed me, what made me happy and what made me want to curl up and die. Once I got a pretty good picture of myself I was able to start making changes. I made some unnecessary changes while I was still trying to get people to like me, and I made some absolutely necessary ones when I realized things that were causing me pain and hardship. What I have continued to do over the years since starting this molding process is get to know ME. It's a continual process and learning project, it never ends! The reward is I have come to understand my needs and wants and learned how to appreciate and love myself.

You cannot ever truly love anyone else until you have learned to love yourself. I thought this was a ridiculous idea until I realized that while breaking my neck to treat others well, love them and help them with their personal needs, I was neglecting myself and destroying myself from the inside out. I wanted so much from people, friends and family. I wanted them to show me all the devotion and attention I showed them. It never happened, because I didn't respect and love myself. I'm telling you, some people can read you like a book, they know when your self -esteem is low or non-existent and they will eat you alive, use you, and abuse you and walk away. You will drive yourself insane trying to recover from all the hurt and betrayals that pile up. Until you open your eyes and stop being a lab rat for others, you will keep piling up disasters. And until you stop allowing yourself to be a lab rat, you can only blame yourself when the disasters occur.

I chose the lab rat as an example because they have no say in what happens to them. They have cancers injected into them, ears grown on them, are subjected to the worst conditions at the whim of scientists and just live or die with things as they come. They have no control over their conditions and no voice, but YOU do!

So here are some questions you might need to ask yourself to see if you are a lab rat and need to escape:

Do you do things that others like to do because it will allow you to be in their company?

Do you do things you don't like when you're with others so you can be in their company?

How often do you change your plans so it will make other people happy?

Do you feel like your choices are not as good as others and change them at the slightest suggestion from others?

Do you seek other people's opinions when making decisions and disregard your inner most thoughts and wishes?

Do you avoid being alone because you aren't content with your own company?

I used to get really depressed because I hardly ever got phone calls. There weren't a bunch of people calling me and asking me to go out with them for social events. I didn't have a gang of girlfriends to hang out with. At the time, there were two females in the house where I was living and both of them were constantly getting phone calls and had events to attend and seemed to be a part of some great social circles. I longed to have that kind of attention and thought about what I needed to do to change things. Then I stopped and thought about what friendship meant to me. I knew that my friends were people I could tell anything and not have to worry about where the information would go. They were people I could depend on when I needed them and vice versa. They were people I never felt would gossip about me behind my back. I had overheard some of the conversations that the other ladies in the house had with their "friends" and realized there was a lot of back stabbing happening. They would talk about one friend and then when that friend called, talk about the other one. It was a vicious cycle and ugly to witness. I realized that I was simply not the type of person that could deal with having lots of friends. I had a small, intimate circle of friends that I didn't need to talk to everyday or go out with all the time to know that they cared about me and valued my friendship. I also realized that I was very comfortable being alone and enjoyed my own company.

I'm not saying that when you have lots of friends that there will definitely be backstabbing and gossiping; there are people who can manage having lots of friends and honor them all. I'm saying that sometimes we see what others have and think we should have it too. We may think that they are better people because they have something we think we need. If you don't ever take the time to get to know who you are and what you need, you will follow roads that weren't meant for you and be lost for a long time. Find and create your own roads, that way you know where you've been and where you want to go.

A stranger asked me once, "Why do you make yourself a slave to others?" I didn't know what he meant at first. Then he explained how I was doing so much for others and very little for myself. It was an eye-opening experience to say the least. He had me do little things to remind myself that I was important and that I was worthy of good things. I realized that it wasn't selfish to love myself and put myself first. I had to put little notes around that house that said, "I'm a star", "I'm worthy", and "To thy own self be true." I felt a little silly at first, seeing these little notes hanging out all around me. But sometimes it's the little things that cause bigger things to happen. You can speak goodness and love into your life. If you say certain things to yourself long enough, you will eventually believe them; that's true for good things as well as bad. So, you want to find all the love you can and speak it into your life and never be afraid, ashamed or embarrassed to love YOU.

Remember and practice:

Whatever you want from others emotionally, make sure you are giving it to yourself first

One of the best friends you can have is yourself, so be a good friend to yourself, listen to your inner self, treat yourself kindly, you deserve it!

Get to it:
- What do you like about yourself: physically, mentally, emotionally, personality-wise, character-wise...?

- What don't you like about yourself? Why? What can you do to change it? Do you not like these things because of something *someone else* said?

- Do you think it's unrealistic to truly love yourself? Is it something you think you can do? Why or why not?

Yep, you guessed it, make a list of likes and dislikes about who you are? Which list is longer? What can be changed immediately? What will take time? How will any of the changes affect you later? How will they affect you right now? And are these changes about YOU and what YOU think, or do you have what someone else may want in mind right now as you think about it?

Work It Out

One of the best things that can happen to me when I'm trying to get things done is to have people that are great at customer service, be it at a restaurant or over the phone or at the doctor's office. So of course, one of the worst things that I have experienced is bad customer service. I don't understand why some people even apply for jobs, and how they end up getting hired when they don't seem to care about how they treat people! I've gone through a drive through and the voice over the speaker is nothing near friendly and I always have to wonder if I want that person dealing with my food. It amazes me how some people go to work and act like they are doing everyone a favor by being there, and that it's ridiculous to expect to get any *work* out of them. They spend time talking on the phone or playing on the computer and then when asked to do their job they get mad! It makes the people that work with them upset because they have to pull their load. People like them usually tend to hang out together, like it's a competition to see who can do the least amount of work. And these people are still getting paid like the people that DO work.

I remember wanting to work really bad when I was in high school. I was given the opportunity to go on interviews and everything, but I didn't have a car and my family wouldn't agree to take me to work or pick me up. It was infuriating! When I got to college I was able to apply for jobs because there was plenty to do near my school. I have had more jobs than I can probably count and at each one I always ran into that person that wanted to just come to work and get paid on payday, but had no intention of really working. They would usually have a plan too; they might do a lot of things that made them look busy but they weren't doing the job they were supposed to be doing. Or they would jump into things when the boss was around, but once they were out of sight, they would switch back to bum mode.

I have a good work ethic. I do the best I can wherever I go so no one can say that I'm lazy. I hate to look bad or be the one that everyone is talking about behind my back. So it always makes me wonder about the lazy people. Do they actually think they are doing the company some benefit, are they not aware of how little work they do, or do they simply not care what people think about them. Some of them do get fired, and they blame the boss, or their coworkers, but never themselves. I just don't know how these people are created. Are they the ones that had a sibling at home that would do all their work and they still got credit for it because the parents didn't know that they weren't working?

I do know that **pride** is at the core of the person that has a good work ethic. They take pride in themselves and they feel awful when they find that they haven't done something to the best standards. If they make a mistake or mess up a situation they learn from it and do what they can to not repeat it. They enjoy the feeling of having done a good job, having helped someone, having made a situation or technique better than it was. Sometimes these people are recognized for their hard work and sometimes they get over looked. But the thing is, they work because they enjoy it and want to be there, and not to gain rewards all the time. Of course it feels good to be recognized for doing well, but sometimes you have to reward yourself, you have to let some little things be your source of reward. For example if you work for a doctor and he rarely if ever tells you that you are doing well, but your patients tell you how much they appreciate you, and you feel good about what you do for them, then your reward lies there. When you go to work your attitude should be that you are working like you would want someone to work if they worked for you. Having faith in God provides a goal that's even greater; you are working to please God and to be able to bless someone else if they come to you with a need.

It's not always about the pay check. Yes you work because you want or need the money, but if you are not a good employee, you may not work very long. And no one owes you anything if your attitude got you fired. As you mature and move into the adult working environment, you will come to find that there are many different kinds of working situations. You'll find that there are people who seem to advance that didn't deserve it, there are people who do just enough and no more, people that go above and beyond and get rewarded and some who do the same but get passed over because they don't have fair bosses. Regardless of the workplace in which you find yourself, do the best you can do, pretend it's your company and be your most valued employee!

Who's the boss...

- Do you have a job or do you have a desire to work?
- If you do work, how would you rate yourself as an employee? Do you listen to directions and follow them or do you roll your eyes and make comments? Do you do your best, or just enough? Do you spend your time doing your assigned tasks or talking to your friends there instead? Are you responsible and on time or early, or do you come in late and expect to get paid like you have been there the entire time? Do you follow the rules and standards or think they are stupid and do what you want? Have you been talked to about your performance

- and given a good rating or told you are in the verge of being let go?
- If you had your own company what kind of people would you want to work for you?
- Have you ever been recognized for doing a good job? How did it make you feel? If you have never been complimented for you work, why do you think that is?
- Do you understand what pride in your work is? Look up pride if you aren't sure and match it to your attitude about your job now or the one you expect to have in the future.

Coming to a close....

So most of these chapters are the order they're in due to my computer putting them in alphabetical order. I guess that's fine because it took away the need for me to organize them myself. I would have had to decide which one was more important and that would have been too hard for me. This chapter is last because recently someone asked me if there was a chapter on bullying. I had to say "No", but the issue was incorporated into many of the chapters which couldn't be helped because I experienced bullying both as a kid and an adult. But now I'm going to attempt to tackle it as a single subject. It will also be a kind of combination chapter because of the impact bullying has had in recent news; suicide. I would have never thought I'd have to address suicide in a book meant for children and young adults but life being what it is, things change and we have to adjust and change with it in order to grow and be successful.

Pushed To The End/The Wrong End

Although I had some pretty rough things happen to me in elementary school it wasn't until I got to 6th grade that things made a drastic change. We moved to a brand new neighborhood and the house we decided to build was put on a lot that the kids used as a playground. The thing is, they had a legitimate, fully stocked, fence enclosed, well-kept playground at the center of the neighborhood. It even had a baseball field. But kids being kids, they chose an empty lot at the back of the neighborhood. Once the building started they would destroy the work that was done, tear things down and break things. It took much longer for our house to be completed of course.

All this was just setting the stage for my introduction to hardship. I was sheltered somewhat at first because we moved during Christmas break so it was cold out. Secondly, I finished the school year at the school I was already attending instead of switching mid-year. But then came the end of the year and I had to face the kids in the hood. Back then kids spent most of their time outside. We had video games, it was just the beginning of that era so being outside was still the norm. When I went out to play and finally started meeting the kids in the neighborhood

all they had to talk about was "Why y'all put your house on our playground?" Like I had some say in this. But it didn't matter to them, I was the enemy. Some older kids were just curious about where I'd come from, but they didn't want to be friends. Then school started. Things just got worse. Now I loved my new school, it was in a pretty area, my teachers were nice, the food was good, there was grass to roll in and I could escape being around kids that didn't like me pretty easily because there was so much area to find hiding spots. But having to ride the bus was the worst part. I got picked on, teased, threatened, my things taken from me and tossed around, pushed and shoved, and talked about. I had to spend about an hour or two alone at home till my family got home from work and these crazy kids would come and throw rocks at the house while I was hunkered down terrified inside….it was just plain stressful.

I was the kid that wasn't athletically talented so I was always picked last for stuff. Almost all of the kids in my new neighborhood were on some sports team or another and gym class was a breeze for them. It was a nightmare for me. So there were certain girls that always targeted me due to my weak physical stature, newness and easily scared nature. One girl decided I'd done something that deserved a whipping and so the classic, "I'm gonna get you after school" threat emerged.

I was never the kind of kid that had physical fights, I avoided this at all costs. So I just didn't know what I was going to do. Finally I told my cousin at home, the one that was seven years older than me. She told me, "You're going to have to fight." I was like "NNoooo.!!!" But she told me that it would be the only way to possibly get things to stop. She told me even if I got beat down I had to at least face them and try. I was a mess. The girl that threatened me came to my house with a group of other girls and rang the doorbell for crying out loud! My aunt was so happy kids were looking for me she cheerfully called me to the door for my dealings with death. I went out to our driveway and it began. She got in my face and did the shoulder push thing and I pushed back, all the while wondering when the first fist would fly. But after 10 or 15 minutes of this I guess the fact that I hadn't run away or cried saved me somehow. The group's attitude changed and something was said that meant I'd be left alone…for the time being.

But there were other tormentors that rose up. They never had any definite reasons for wanting to torture me, they just knew they could so they did. They embarrassed me in the hallways of the school, they taunted me with just their words and physical prowess. I couldn't escape, they would pop up when I least expected it and say something that made everyone laugh. No matter what good thing I may have succeeded at, they found a way to make it look like a joke. I hated these girls, but somehow I survived it all. I took pride in not being like them and enjoyed the things that made me happy. I appreciated the kids that left me alone or that didn't laugh at the mean things that happened to me. I excelled in my classes because I loved learning and enjoyed the reward of having my teachers recognize my achievements. Nothing those rotten kids did kept me from succeeding.

Here's one of the triumphs I experienced. There was a ceremony for all the Seniors who had received scholarships for college. I walked into a room full of kids with athletic scholarships, there were a few with ones for academic, but the majority were sports related. Most were the same kids that had bullied me. They turned and looked at me and asked what I was doing there. I told them, "I got full scholarship." They had no idea that although I couldn't shoot basketball well, did horribly at Volleyball, failed Dance Team and Drill Team tryout, and got cut from the track team simply because I wasn't one of the coaches favorites, that I was on the Honor Roll every year and had taken more classes than I actually needed to graduate. Many of them had partial scholarships, I had a full ride, meaning everything was paid for, for 4 years or until I graduated so long as I kept the grade point average that was required. It was amazing to see their faces when my name was called and my scholarship detailed.

Today's bullies are a whole different type of creature. I had to navigate my bullies on a pretty level playing field, at school or on the bus or in the streets of our neighborhood. Now kids have the Internet to do their deeds; fast access to hundreds of eyes and ears. You can wake up to a rumor having spread overnight to the entire world, or what you feel is the world. Your encounters with bullies are filmed and posted. Your humiliations are replayed again and again in person and online.

How do you combat this? How do you protect yourself? How do you survive 4 years or more of this kind of insanity? I don't have any clear-cut answers. I only have suggestions and advice.

The fuel and energy of a bully is fear, your fear. When they know they can scare someone, they take full advantage of it. If they are bigger or stronger or even just think they are, they use this as a weapon as well. We've all seen the movies, read the books, seen or experienced first-hand the scrawny kid that is tormented by kids or kids that are bigger than them. This is such a difficult situation. They smaller kid most often feels they have no options to protect themselves and are subject to these assaults on a regular basis. This situation is worse when a bully team is involved; more than one kid committing the assaults.

My suggestions for this situation are:
1. Tell your school administrators. I know, no one likes a "snitch". But if it's going to keep you from being assaulted, it's worth being called names instead.
2. Take a self-defense course. If your family can afford this it would be great, but there are beginning to be more of these courses offered at no cost in the community as the need for it arises.

3. Run. Yes, this seems like a cowardly thing. But it's not, it's a survival thing. My uncle once told me that if I was ever in a situation where someone was coming after me and I knew I wasn't prepared, to run! The second part of his advice was to come back with some form of weapon...like a brick or rock, broken bottle etc. I got his intent but I felt like just getting away was good enough. I wouldn't come back to insight another altercation, but if confronted and there were things around me that I could use to protect myself then yes, bricks and rocks would be welcomed.
4. Keep some form of alarm on your person. These are inexpensive; whistles, air horns, personal protection alarms that are really loud. If pepper spray is legal in your area, have some with you at all times. If you can't get this, insect repellent that sprays in a stream is just as effective and it has a further reach!
5. Scream....LOUD! Act "crazy"...do things that will confuse and throw off your attackers. Who would beat up someone that's already laying on the ground shaking and flipping around in fits? This may sound ridiculous...but if it works, you keep yourself safe!
6. Never travel alone. If you walk home, don't walk alone. Find other kids that you can travel with and have a safe, easily seen route home. Don't allow yourself to be trapped in areas that you can't escape. Stay on streets that are well traveled by other people.

In a nutshell you have to do what you need to keep yourself safe and find ways to determine what the best action is for the situation. Sometimes you don't need to do anything. By this I mean your reaction to some things determines an outcome. I read someplace that when a small child is acting out it's to get attention. If the parent gives the child attention during these tantrums the strange thing is the kid typically starts acting worse! But if the parent simply ignores the behavior, the child isn't getting the reaction they anticipated and they stop acting a fool. Same with accidents like falls or other bumbles. Kid falls down, not hard, no skin is broken. The parent comes running making a big scene out of it, kid starts crying because of the parent's reaction to the fall. I've seen kids fall and the first thing they do is look around, they aren't sure how to react. If an adult says, it's okay, you're ok, they just dust themselves off and keep playing!

So I think this can be applied to the work of bullies. If what they do gets no attention from you, they don't get the desired effect, so they don't repeat the actions. If you aren't physically hurt by their actions you can walk away and live another day. If the bullying takes the form of cyber tactics (Facebook, etc.) now what? Okay, what was said? Was it true? Was it totally fabricated? Either way, has it REALLY hurt you, or just your feelings. I don't mean to say that hurt feelings don't mean anything but in the big picture, how does what was said weigh in your life? Could you just let it go with the understanding that it's something falsely presented with the desire to hurt you? Knowing that you aren't truly hurt takes the power away from the attack and attacker.

The thing with bullies is they are really the ones that are hurting. I know you're like "Yeah right!" but it's true. Hurt people, hurt people. They are attempting to feel better by projecting the hurt onto someone else. Am I asking you to feel sorry for them? Not really, I'm just saying that sometimes people like this don't even know why they are doing what they do. They just act on what they feel is power. You have to decide how much power you want to give them.

I've made this sound relatively simple I know. I don't want to make you feel your sense of hurt and anger is devalued however. I have felt the sting of being bullied, felt powerless and small. But like I said...I survived! I had more things to look forward to during those times that the damage bullies inflicted wasn't the primary focus of my life, they were an unfortunate annoyance. And in the end, I achieved goals I'd set, met people that were kind to me, learned how to defend myself in time and lived a happy and healthy life.

A key word here is....LIVED. So now for the second part of this chapter. The "wrong end" part. Wrong end being, suicide. This is the worst way to attempt to end your struggles, pain, torment, anger, sadness, and feeling of hopelessness or powerlessness. Suicide is a permanent answer to a temporary problem. I would never had thought I'd have to address suicide to children. Never imagined hearing that a child had taken their lives. Now I'm not going to pretend that the thought never crossed my mind either, even when I was a child. I can admit that there was a time when I questioned my worth in life. I suffered from the death of my parents by age 3, abuse from extended family, bullies at school, sexual molestation by a family member, and feelings of not being loved or wanted. I laid in bed one day and thought, "I may as well be dead." But as soon as I thought this, my heart started racing! It was like I had spoken a curse out loud and created a shift in the universe! I think what I'd actually done was upset God. I think He shook me by grasping my heart in His hand and saying, I made you...for a reason...and it's not your life to contemplate taking.

I think I've illustrated in this work that I was the kind of kid that didn't like to be in trouble. Although I did plenty of things to get into trouble, they were not significant, nothing that could have gotten me into jail or anything. I was a teacher's pet, and after suffering from the embarrassment of being put in a lower level class after abusing a priviledge one of my teachers had given me, I stopped being such a class clown. So, the thought of making GOD made, was a little much.

So I ask you, what do you think suicide would solve? It might take you away from the torment of bullies or other things in your life you feel are overwhelming. But it also takes away the opportunity for you to learn to rise above hurts, abuses and other bad things that happen to most people while they live and grow older. If everyone that was struggling with something took their lives, there wouldn't be very many people left on Earth. We are created with the strength of the Universe, Jesus, God…inside us. Yet many people fail to recognize the strengths they have. They are often tricked into thinking that they are powerless and so they allow others to ruin what could be happy, fulfilling lives. It makes me sad to hear that so many people turn to drugs, alcohol and other unhealthy things just to escape everyday life. They spend their days in a fog of unreality rather than harnessing the powers they have within to move past the obstacles place in front of them. The unhealthy habits many times lead to death, so it's like suicide, stretch out over time.

Whatever you are going through, there is a solution. You owe it to yourself to give it the effort of finding a solution before opting to take your life. You were placed on this Earth for a reason. It may take you many years to figure out what the reason is, but it's the journey that's most important; the things you will learn along the way that help you become the best person you can be. So that's your goal in a way, to wrestle with whatever comes knowing you have a better self to look forward to in the future. Do you want to meet your Best Self? Then you will have to wait, deal with the bullies, deal with the pressures and disappointments, listen to your inner self and trust that God has a plan for you and will give you answers if you ASK for them.

Life can be hard. But it's worth living.

Finally...

So that's it ladies. I think I'm done. I know that I will go back and read this and think, "Oh man! I wish I'd say this or that instead!" Or, "Oh no, I forgot to mention this or that!" But that's ok, because it will provide me material for either the updated version of this or a brand new project. I began this project many years ago and yet reading back through it I have been able to bless myself all over again. The information needed to be freshened in my spirit again as it is helpful even with situations I am dealing with right now! All I really want is for this to help you either a little, or a lot. I want it to make a difference in your life. I want it to be a tool you use for many years to come and that you share what you have learned from it with someone you love, a friend, family member and even a stranger. Before I leave this Earth I want to be able to touch as many girls, ladies, women as possible that are struggling with life and help them move past the hurts and harms the best ways they can in order to experience and enjoy all the GOOD that this life has to offer. As I said, I'm no expert! I am still struggling through life myself. But I know that God has a plan for me and I see his blessings new each day. He has trusted me to be in a position to give a helping hand to those around me and I am extending it to you with sincere, and genuine LOVE.

ABOUT THE AUTHOR

Sonja Reynolds has lived in more places than she can recall to finally settle in Colorado. She loves animals, children, messy snacks, chilly weather, reading books from start to finish and thrift store shopping. Her greatest wish is to find the best parts of everyone she meets and be remembered for her genuine desire to help others learn to love themselves.